LOOKING AT TYPE SERIES

Looking at Type and Careers

by Charles R. Martin, Ph.D.

This publication was funded in part by a grant from the Human Resource Research Institute, Tokyo, Japan.

CENTER FOR APPLICATIONS OF PSYCHOLOGICAL TYPE, INC.
GAINESVILLE, FLORIDA

Copyright 1995 Center for Applications of Psychological Type

All rights reserved. No part of this book, except as specifically noted below, may be reproduced in any form or by any electronic or mechanical means including information storage and retrieval systems without permission in writing from the publisher (CAPT). Exceptions: A reviewer may quote brief passages in a review.

Published by
Center for Applications of Psychological Type, Inc.
2815 NW 13th Street, Suite 401
Gainesville, FL 32609-2815
(904) 375-0160

Edited by Thomas C. Thompson, Ph.D.

The publisher gratefully acknowledges the assistance of Production Ink, Gainesville, Florida, for the design, production, and printing of this title.

Looking at Type is a trademark of the Center for Applications of Psychological Type, Inc., Gainesville, FL.

Myers-Briggs Type Indicator and MBTI are registered trademarks of Consulting Psychologists Press, Inc., Palo Alto, CA.

Printed in the United States of America.

ISBN 0-935652-25-6

Acknowledgements

For her ongoing support and presence in my life, and for her wisdom and insight into people, I want to express gratitude to my wife and life partner, Tamara.

I would also like to express appreciation to the wide range of people who contributed knowledge, editorial review, and support during the development and completion of this project. Thanks go to Tom Thompson, Ron Walsh and colleagues, and Jamelyn Delong for their reviews of the manuscript and their helpful comments. Special thanks go to Mary McCaulley and Jerry Macdaid, whose extensive knowledge and experience with type, and whose willingness to share those, helped make this book possible. Their presence, support, and belief in me has helped me to create a career that is an extension of who I am.

Acknowledgement also goes to the intellectual legacy and person of Isabel Myers, whose groundbreaking work formed the basis for the applications of type described in this book. Finally, acknowledgement and appreciation go to the countless friends, colleagues, and clients who have contributed both directly and indirectly to the development of this book.

Contents

Foreword vii
Introduction ix
Looking at Yourself 1
   The MBTI and the Basic Language of Type 1
   Values, Interests, and Skills 7
      Your Values 7
      Your Interests 9
      Your Skills 10
   Type Dynamics and Development 12
      Your Type Dynamics 12
      Your Type Development 15
Looking at Careers 19
   ISTJ 19
   ISFJ 22
   INFJ 25
   INTJ 27
   ISTP 30
   ISFP 32
   INFP 35
   INTP 38
   ESTP 41
   ESFP 43
   ENFP 46
   ENTP 49
   ESTJ 52
   ESFJ 54
   ENFJ 57
   ENTJ 60
   Gathering More Information 64
Looking at Decisions 67
Looking at What's Next 71
   Setting Goals and Taking Action 71
   Selling Your Differences 75
Further Resources 77

V
LOOKING AT TYPE AND CAREERS

Foreword

This book is intended for those who want to use psychological type in their career exploration. A variety of people will find it helpful: high school and college students considering a first-time job, young adults who are already working and who want to find out more about career options, and adults who may have been working in a career for several years but who want or need to consider a career change.

People invest an enormous amount of time and energy in their work. Thus, the ideal situation is to be involved in a career that is rewarding, enjoyable and which makes use of one's natural talents. Type can help you find just such a career.

A quick review of the Myers-Briggs Type Indicator (MBTI)® and type theory is provided in this book, but if you need more information, *Gifts Differing* provides an excellent introduction to these topics.

In the pages that follow, type will be used to help you understand yourself and your natural preferences, and how those preferences relate to your career exploration. You will also see that type differences are all valuable and that no combination of type preferences is better than any other combination of preferences. Each of the sixteen types has its own strengths and potential blindspots, and in this book you will see how you can make use of your strengths and work through your blindspots. Many people find that upon discovering their true type there is a feeling of "fit" and a sense of relief as they understand that their likes and dislikes, ways of interacting, goals and behaviors are all natural extensions of their combination of preferences. Type can also help you find this sense of "fit" in your career.

As you read this book, remember that you are the expert on who you are and what your type preferences are, and you are the one who will decide how you will express your type in whatever career you choose. We wish you the best in your career exploration.

Myers-Briggs Type Indicator and MBTI are registered trademarks of Consulting Psychologists Press, Palo Alto, CA.

Introduction

Isabel Myers' earliest goal for the MBTI was to help people choose careers that would be interesting to them and would call on their strengths. Ongoing research with individuals and the MBTI has confirmed that there are very real type differences in how people learn and how they work. Research has also clearly shown there are patterns in the types of people who tend to choose or to avoid different occupations. You will be introduced to these patterns later in this book.

The bottom line for the application of psychological type in your career exploration is expressed in two phrases often used by Isabel Myers: "Gifts Differing," and "The Constructive Use of Differences."

The four sections of this book address four major areas of career exploration. Essentially, you need to gather information on yourself, you need to gather information on careers, you need to make decisions, and you need to follow through on the decisions you have made. This book is designed to help you understand and make use of type at every one of these four steps.

As you read this book, you will want to respect your own natural tendencies, and explore careers in a way that makes use of the strengths of your type. In addition, you will also want to have a healthy respect for the weaknesses or blindspots that can be associated with your particular type preferences.

The bottom line is that you should approach this book in a way that works for you, while considering that the parts and activities you most want to skip may be of particular use to someone with your type preferences.

Looking at Yourself

Looking at yourself means gaining some understanding of who you are through an exploration of five dimensions of life that are important in successful career choices. These five dimensions are: (1) personality type, (2) values, (3) interests, (4) skills, and (5) type dynamics and development. You will be introduced to each of these five dimensions in this book.

The MBTI and the Basic Language of Type

In this first section you will learn more about the MBTI and the four preferences that are the basis for your personality type.

Each question on the MBTI provides equally valuable choices and asks you to indicate which appeals to you more. The questions let you indicate a preference on four dichotomous (either/or) scales: extraversion versus introversion, sensing versus intuition, thinking versus feeling, and judging versus perceiving. There are no right or wrong answers; they simply represent preferences. When the MBTI is scored, the combination of preferences on the four scales indicates one of sixteen types.

Below, these four basic preference pairs of type theory and the MBTI will be explained. On each scale, there are two different choices, or preferences. Everyone uses both choices at one time or another, but each person naturally prefers one of the choices over the other, just as people are naturally right-handed or left-handed.

As you read the descriptions of the four pairs of preferences below, see if you can recognize which of each pair is your most natural preference.

1 LOOKING AT TYPE AND CAREERS

2 LOOKING AT TYPE AND CAREERS

Direction of Energy: Extraversion (E) or Introversion (I)

"Extravert" comes from the Latin for "outward turning." When we are extraverting, our energy goes out to the world around us. The outer world draws our attention and interest. We notice what is happening, and like to jump into action.

Introversion comes from the Latin for "inward turning." When we are introverting, our energy goes inward toward the concepts and ideas that help explain the world around us. The inner world draws our attention and interest. We want a clear idea of what is happening before we move into action.

Below are examples of qualities and behaviors often associated with extraverting and introverting. Check any that apply to you.

EXTRAVERSION — People with a preference for extraversion...

- ☐ Direct energy mostly to the people and things in the "outside world."
- ☐ May find that other activities can disturb their concentration. They may also like involvement in many activities.
- ☐ Like to work on the action plan in a problem-solving group.
- ☐ Are often drawn to work with high people contact, out-of-office activities, and variety.
- ☐ Are attracted to careers where action and interaction are important, such as business, sales/marketing, personal services, food services, public relations, and government.

INTROVERSION — People with a preference for introversion...

- ☐ Direct energy mostly to the ideas in their minds.
- ☐ May find that they can concentrate for long periods of time. They may like focusing on one activity in depth and dislike interruptions.
- ☐ Like to work on the conceptual framework in a problem-solving group.
- ☐ Are often drawn to work requiring solo activities or one-to-one contact, continuity, and concentration.
- ☐ Are attracted to careers where ideas are important, such as college teaching, science, research, library work, computers, mechanical work, electronics, and engineering.

Given that you sometimes extravert and sometimes introvert, does a natural preference for extraversion or introversion fit you better?

Extraversion (E) ____   Introversion (I) ____

3
LOOKING AT TYPE AND CAREERS

The Tools of Perception: Sensing (S) and Intuition (N)

In type theory, there are two primary ways of taking in information: sensing and intuition. People tend to trust one of these kinds of information over the other. Your preference for sensing perception or intuitive perception can have an effect on which careers you tend to enjoy.

Sensing is the tool of the mind that deals with the present reality. Sensing refers to the information we take in with our senses — what we see, hear, smell, touch, and taste, as well as the kinesthetics of our bodies. Individuals with a preference for sensing often develop excellent powers of observation, and may also develop gifts of reality, practicality, common sense, and working in the here-and-now.

Intuition is the opposite kind of perception from sensing.

Below are examples of qualities and behaviors that often come from preferring and developing either sensing perception or intuitive perception. Check any that apply to you.

SENSING PERCEPTION — People with a preference for sensing...

- ☐ Are often seen as realistic and practical, and good at grasping the facts and details.
- ☐ Focus more on the present than the future.
- ☐ Are often patient and careful with precise work and routine, and they like the chance to hone a skill.
- ☐ Tend to seek education that has practical uses. They are more likely to prefer hands-on training.
- ☐ Are attracted to careers where they can be involved in production, management of a business or service, construction, office details and accounting, patient care, police and military, and similar hands-on activities to solve immediate problems.

INTUITIVE PERCEPTION — People with a preference for intuition...

- ☐ Are often seen as imaginative and insightful, and good at grasping the big picture.
- ☐ Focus more on the future than on the present.
- ☐ Are often patient in projects with many intangibles and possibilities, and they enjoy new ways of doing things.
- ☐ Tend to value knowledge for its own sake. They are more likely to seek higher education.
- ☐ Are attracted to careers where communication or theory are important, as in counseling, journalism, teaching, writing and art, religion, science, research, law, or areas where long-range planning in business or policy development are required.

Given that we use both sensing and intuition everyday, does a natural preference for sensing or intuition fit you better?

Sensing (S) ____   Intuition (N) ____

4
LOOKING AT TYPE AND CAREERS

Intuition is the tool of the mind that lets us see beyond the present and imagine what has never been before. It lets us deal with symbols and abstractions. Individuals with a preference for intuition often develop skills of imagination, and may also develop gifts in working with symbols, meanings, patterns and in seeing possibilities.

The Tools of Judgment: Thinking (T) and Feeling (F)

When we have established from our sensing tool what is, and from our intuitive tool what might be, it is time to use our judgment to make decisions for action. There are two tools for making decisions — thinking and feeling.

Thinking judgment is an impersonal tool for making decisions. It approaches the problem objectively,

---

Below are examples of qualities and behaviors that often come from preferring and developing either thinking judgment or feeling judgment. Check any that apply to you.

THINKING JUDGMENT — People with a preference for thinking...

- ☐ Prefer to understand experience through logical thinking.
- ☐ Seek objective truth and fairness, regardless of effects, and may be seen as forthright and firm.
- ☐ Naturally critique to detect errors or inconsistencies.
- ☐ Are often drawn to education in fields where logical analysis and an objective approach to objects, ideas, numbers, or persons are the focus. However, they are found in all fields of education.
- ☐ Are often attracted to careers in skilled trades and crafts, science and technology, computers, production, management, law, police, and criminal justice work.

FEELING JUDGMENT — People with a preference for feeling...

- ☐ Prefer to understand experience in the context of human relationships.
- ☐ Seek harmony and cooperation, sometimes ignoring the consequences, and may be seen as warm and understanding.
- ☐ Naturally appreciate the merits of others.
- ☐ Are often drawn to education in fields where communication and a more personal approach to, and involvement with, people and ideas are the focus. However, they are found in all fields of education.
- ☐ Are often attracted to careers in teaching, health care, clerical and office work, personal and human services, communication, entertainment, counseling, and the ministry.

Given that we all use both thinking and feeling at times, does a natural preference for thinking judgment or feeling judgment fit you better?

Thinking (T) _____   Feeling (F) _____

from an outside point of view. Thinking uses logical analysis to determine likely cause-and-effect outcomes of the possible options. It puts choices in a rational order on the basis of consequences, often with the goal of finding out what is objectively "true."

Feeling judgment is a more personal tool for making decisions. Feeling is concerned with what matters — the long-term good and the short-term good. Feeling reaches decisions by weighing the values of various options, and by putting what people care about in the forefront. In the MBTI feeling does not mean emotion. Feeling puts choices in a rational order, based on a continuum of more to less valuable, often with the goal of determining what is "important."

5 LOOKING AT TYPE AND CAREERS

Two Orientations to the World: Judging (J) and Perceiving (P)

There are two different lifestyle orientations to the outer world — judging and perceiving. Everyone goes back and forth between perceiving and judging, but perceiving types stay longer in the information-

---

Below are examples of qualities and behaviors that are often associated with a preference for either judgment or perception. Check any that apply to you.

THE JUDGING LIFESTYLE — People with a preference for judgment...

- ☐ Value order, structure, and predictability, and like the completion of tasks.

- ☐ Want matters decided and settled, and take deadlines and schedules seriously.

- ☐ Tolerate, and may even enjoy, routine.
- ☐ Are often found in management jobs.

- ☐ Are attracted to work settings where plans, system, order, and deadlines are important, and they are often drawn to tasks where they can assume responsibility.

THE PERCEIVING LIFESTYLE — People with a preference for perception...

- ☐ Value spontaneity and the challenge of dealing with the unexpected, and don't want to rush to closure.

- ☐ Like to leave options open and may let other interesting developments interfere with deadlines.

- ☐ Find routine boring, even intolerable.
- ☐ Are often found in trouble-shooting jobs.

- ☐ Are attracted to work settings where change, flexibility and innovation are important, and they are often drawn to tasks where they can work independently.

Given that our lifestyles reflect both judging and perceiving at times, does a natural preference for a judging lifestyle or a perceiving lifestyle fit you better?

Judging (J) ____   Perceiving (P) ____

LOOKING AT TYPE AND CAREERS

gathering mode, while judging types move more quickly to the decision-making mode. As a result, perceiving types often look more flexible, open, and adaptable, while judging types often look more structured, organized, and closure-seeking.

Clarifying Your Preferences

Often people are not clear about what they like, but are more clear about what they don't like or what is stressful for them. If you are having difficulty figuring out your type preferences, you can ask yourself the following kinds of questions:

(1) If I had to choose, would it more difficult for me to work with a group of people all day (E), or to work alone all day (I)?

(2) Would it be more stressful for me to continually pay attention to the facts and realities all of the time (S), or to continually come up with new ideas (N)?

(3) Is it more difficult for me to constantly step outside the situation and analyze it impersonally (T), or to be continually concerned with the impact of events on individuals in my life (F)?

(4) If I had to choose, would it be more stressful for me to adhere to a schedule during the day, even one I created (J), or to continually have to adapt to changing work conditions (P)?

At this point, try to make a decision about what your four type preferences are and note them in the spaces below.

My preferences are:

___ ___ ___ ___
E or I   S or N   T or F   J or P

Write a brief statement about what your preferences may mean for your career choice. You might want to discuss this with someone who also knows type.

_____
_____
_____
_____

7 LOOKING AT TYPE AND CAREERS

Values, Interests, and Skills

As we have said, your MBTI type provides you with the first basic dimension for looking at yourself. The MBTI, however, is only a part of the larger process of self-understanding. In their exploration of careers, individuals also need to be concerned with some other dimensions: their values, interests, skills, and the dynamics of their type.

Your Values

Values are those enduring characteristics or aspects of life and work that we consider important, even essential, to our satisfaction. What motivates you and would make a career worthwhile? In other words, what makes you get up in the morning?

There are often relationships between a person's type preferences and the kinds of values that person holds. However, it should be understood that knowledge of your values should also *add* to information gained from knowledge of your psychological type. Thus, if you are an ESTJ, you may be inclined to share some values with other ESTJs, but you will also differ in values from other ESTJs. Psychological type is not a pigeon hole, and two ESTJs can differ widely in career paths based on differences in their values.

At this point, take a moment to reflect on what things are important for you as you think about a career. What do you value? What motivates you? Knowledge of your values helps refine your understanding of who you are and what you want. For example, an ENFJ whose highest values are creativity, recognition, and self-expression might consider an acting career. In this fashion, the ENFJ's values are met, and they can utilize their natural preferences. On the other hand, an ENFJ whose highest values are family, spirituality, and nurturing others might be more satisfied in a career in the clergy rather than in acting, or some other setting where they can attend to the spiritual and emotional needs of others.

8
LOOKING AT TYPE AND CAREERS

Below, write your highest ranked values, and how this information adds to or clarifies your understanding of yourself, potential work settings, and careers you may be considering. How might you pursue them? You may also want to discuss these with someone else.

_____
_____
_____
_____
_____

As you read through the following list of values, check the ones that are most important to you, and decide which are your top values.

VALUES CHECKLIST

- ☐ Achievement
- ☐ Aesthetics
- ☐ Affiliation
- ☐ Autonomy/independence
- ☐ Challenge
- ☐ Comfort
- ☐ Competition
- ☐ Contributing to society
- ☐ Creativity
- ☐ Enjoyment
- ☐ Ethics
- ☐ Excitement/adventure
- ☐ Expertise
- ☐ Fame
- ☐ Family
- ☐ Friendship
- ☐ Health

- ☐ Helping others
- ☐ Honesty
- ☐ Inner harmony
- ☐ Intellectual pursuits
- ☐ Job environment
- ☐ Leadership
- ☐ Leisure time
- ☐ Location/geography
- ☐ Loyalty
- ☐ Money and/or wealth
- ☐ Nurturing others
- ☐ Order/structure
- ☐ Physically demanding
- ☐ Play
- ☐ Power/authority
- ☐ Prestige/recognition
- ☐ Producing something
- ☐ Public contact

- ☐ Respect
- ☐ Responsibility
- ☐ Security
- ☐ Self-actualization
- ☐ Service (social or other)
- ☐ Spirituality
- ☐ Stability
- ☐ Status
- ☐ Supportive environment
- ☐ Time spent at work
- ☐ Variety
- ☐ Working alone
- ☐ Working with others

Other values not listed
- ☐ _____
- ☐ _____
- ☐ _____
- ☐ _____

LOOKING AT TYPE AND CAREERS

Your Interests

Your interests are those areas of work and/or study that naturally attract you. Interests include the kinds of tasks you like, the areas of thought that engage you, and the occupational areas that excite you.

On the following page you can make an informal assessment of your interests, or you may have already taken an interest inventory. It's important to remember that for some individuals, information from the MBTI and their interest assessment may clearly agree, while for others the information may not appear to agree. Remember, every ESTJ is like every other ESTJ, like some other ESTJs, and like no other ESTJ. Whether the MBTI and interest assessments appear to agree or not, a fuller picture of who you are is the result.

At this point, stop and look through the list of career interest areas on page 11. What are your top areas? As you go through the list, don't worry about whether or not you have the skills for that area. For now, just mark your areas of interest.

Here again, knowledge of your interests helps broaden your sense of who you are. For example, a person with type preferences of ISTJ may have interests in the physical sciences, research, and teaching. Though teaching might not be predicted on the basis of type alone, this new information must be considered in looking at possible careers. This ISTJ might consider teaching physics or chemistry in a university. Another ISTJ who has interests in business, mathematics, and finance might rather consider a career in accounting. Though these are overly simple examples, we see that each person is considering a career where they could make good use of their type preferences as well.

If your type preferences and interest areas seem very inconsistent, you may want to ask yourself some of the following kinds of questions.

1) What might be the source of the inconsistency? Have my family, life experiences, and environment influenced my interests?

2) Are the results ultimately inconsistent, or might they be usefully integrated? For example, could I find a way of working in a career interest area that would allow me to make use of my natural preferences?

10
LOOKING AT TYPE AND CAREERS

Below, write which are your top interest areas, and a brief statement about how each of these areas interests you. What do these areas mean for your career exploration? You may find it helpful to discuss these areas with someone else.

_____
_____
_____
_____
_____

Your Skills

The next dimension involves looking at your skills. You can also think of these as your abilities, talents, gifts, or competencies. Skills are what you use in your life and in a career to accomplish things, to reach certain goals. Skills enable you to reach those things you consider valuable.

Think about skills you have that can be transfered from one job to another. For example, you may have edited a high school newspaper and organized a small staff of three in doing so. The transferable skills that you learned from that job include interviewing, writing, editing, organizing people, and leading. These skills can be applied in any number of careers you may be considering, whether the career involves newspaper editing, sales, politics, running a business, or work in the social sciences.

A note about type: As you exercise your type preferences, it is likely that you will naturally develop some skills over others. For example, people who prefer judging may be more inclined than people who prefer perceiving to develop organizing skills. However, people who prefer perceiving can develop excellent skills in organizing, but they may be less inclined to do so, or they may be less satisfied in a career that requires them to constantly use their organizing skills. Remember also that skills can be learned and developed with practice, hence you don't have to be limited by lack of skill in an area.

Look at the Interests and Skills table on the following page and check any of the areas in which you have skills. Check those areas in which you can perform more or less competently and don't worry now whether or not you have an interest in that area. Be honest with yourself about your skill level. You may also find it helpful to note any of the skills that you

11
LOOKING AT TYPE AND CAREERS

would like to develop.

Skills also provide additional information whether they appear to be consistent or inconsistent with your type preferences. For example, an introvert who has more skills (and interests) in working with people

---

As you read through the list, place checks in the "Interest" boxes next to any areas that naturally attract you.

INTEREST AND SKILL AREAS

Interest / Skill

- ☐ ☐ Adventure
- ☐ ☐ Advertising/marketing
- ☐ ☐ Agriculture
- ☐ ☐ Animal care
- ☐ ☐ Architecture
- ☐ ☐ Art/design
- ☐ ☐ Athletics/physical fitness
- ☐ ☐ Biology
- ☐ ☐ Business
- ☐ ☐ Business management
- ☐ ☐ Coaching
- ☐ ☐ Computer sciences
- ☐ ☐ Cooking
- ☐ ☐ Counseling
- ☐ ☐ Crafts/trades
- ☐ ☐ Creating
- ☐ ☐ Data management
- ☐ ☐ Drama
- ☐ ☐ Economics
- ☐ ☐ Engineering
  - ☐ ☐ Aeronautical
  - ☐ ☐ Chemical
  - ☐ ☐ Civil
  - ☐ ☐ Electrical
  - ☐ ☐ Mechanical
- ☐ ☐ English
- ☐ ☐ Farming
- ☐ ☐ Fashion

- ☐ ☐ Finance
- ☐ ☐ Foreign languages
- ☐ ☐ Forestry
- ☐ ☐ Group work or activities
- ☐ ☐ Healing
- ☐ ☐ Home economics
- ☐ ☐ Humanities
- ☐ ☐ International activities
- ☐ ☐ Inventing
- ☐ ☐ Law
- ☐ ☐ Law enforcement
- ☐ ☐ Leadership
- ☐ ☐ Management
- ☐ ☐ Mathematics
- ☐ ☐ Mechanical activities
- ☐ ☐ Medicine
  - ☐ ☐ Research
  - ☐ ☐ Practice
- ☐ ☐ Military
- ☐ ☐ Music
- ☐ ☐ Music education
- ☐ ☐ Office work
- ☐ ☐ Outdoor work
- ☐ ☐ Performing
- ☐ ☐ Physical education
- ☐ ☐ Physical sciences

- ☐ ☐ Planning
- ☐ ☐ Plants or gardens
- ☐ ☐ Politics
- ☐ ☐ Psychology
  - ☐ ☐ Research
  - ☐ ☐ Practice
- ☐ ☐ Public Speaking
- ☐ ☐ Reading
- ☐ ☐ Sales
- ☐ ☐ Social sciences
- ☐ ☐ Social service
- ☐ ☐ Religious/spiritual activities
- ☐ ☐ Sociology
- ☐ ☐ Supervision
- ☐ ☐ Teaching
  - ☐ ☐ Preschool
  - ☐ ☐ Elementary
  - ☐ ☐ HighSchool
  - ☐ ☐ University
- ☐ ☐ Training
- ☐ ☐ Woodworking
- ☐ ☐ Writing

Other areas not listed
- ☐ ☐ _____
- ☐ ☐ _____
- ☐ ☐ _____
- ☐ ☐ _____

12 LOOKING AT TYPE AND CAREERS

may be more satisfied in a career in teaching, whereas an introvert who has more skills (and interests) in technical data-oriented areas may be more satisfied in a career in computer science.

Below, write which skills are the most important to you and which appear reasonably well developed. You may also want to write down skills that you would like to develop. What do these skill areas mean for your career exploration? You might find it helpful to talk about these skills with someone else.

_____
_____
_____
_____
_____

Type Dynamics and Development

You have been introduced to four of the five dimensions of self-understanding: your type, values, interests, and skills. At this point we want to return to type for the final dimension: your type dynamics and type development.

Your Type Dynamics

The four functions are the building blocks of your type. Everyone needs and uses the four basic mental functions: sensing, intuition, thinking, and feeling. People simply prefer to focus on some rather than others, and prefer them in a particular order. This is what is meant when we refer to type dynamics. The type table in this section shows the order of preference each of the sixteen types has for the four functions: sensing, intuition, thinking, and feeling.

One of the two middle letters of your type is your favorite function (also called your dominant). Look at the chart to see which is your favorite. When you are doing work that uses your favorite function, you will feel the most competent and sure of yourself, and the work will likely feel easier and more natural.

The other of the two middle letters of your type is your second favorite function (also called the auxiliary). This function tends to be the second most well developed and lends balance to your dominant function. Work that uses your second favorite function also tends to feel easier and more natural.

13
LOOKING AT TYPE AND CAREERS

Since your dominant and auxiliary functions are your most preferred functions, and usually the most well developed, they tend to be *the most* important as you think about career exploration. They tend to tell you what you will find motivating in a career and what skills you will most easily develop. For example, if intuition (N) and feeling (F) are your two most favored functions, then you will probably be more inclined to focus on the possibilities, the future, and have concern for harmony, and you might find it relatively easy to develop skills with symbols or skills in working with people. NFs are indeed often found in careers that draw on these qualities (e.g., the arts, counseling, writing). You might also have more difficulty developing interest or skills in using your sensing and thinking, because these are the opposites of your natural preferences. NFs are found much less often in careers that draw on the qualities often associated with sensing and thinking (e.g., management,

ISTJ	ISFJ	INFJ	INTJ
1) Sensing (Dominant) – I	1) Sensing (Dominant) – I	1) Intuition (Dominant) – I	1) Intuition (Dominant) – I
2) Thinking (Auxiliary) – E	2) Feeling (Auxiliary) – E	2) Feeling (Auxiliary) – E	2) Thinking (Auxiliary) – E
3) Feeling (Tertiary) – E	3) Thinking (Tertiary) – E	3) Thinking (Tertiary) – E	3) Feeling (Tertiary) – E
4) Intuition (Inferior) – E	4) Intuition (Inferior) – E	4) Sensing (Inferior) – E	4) Sensing (Inferior) – E
ISTP	**ISFP**	**INFP**	**INTP**
1) Thinking (Dominant) – I	1) Feeling (Dominant) – I	1) Feeling (Dominant) – I	1) Thinking (Dominant) – I
2) Sensing (Auxiliary) – E	2) Sensing (Auxiliary) – E	2) Intuition (Auxiliary) – E	2) Intuition (Auxiliary) – E
3) Intuition (Tertiary) – E	3) Intuition (Tertiary) – E	3) Sensing (Tertiary) – E	3) Sensing (Tertiary) – E
4) Feeling (Inferior) – E	4) Thinking (Inferior) – E	4) Thinking (Inferior) – E	4) Feeling (Inferior) – E
ESTP	**ESFP**	**ENFP**	**ENTP**
1) Sensing (Dominant) – E	1) Sensing (Dominant) – E	1) Intuition (Dominant) – E	1) Intuition (Dominant) – E
2) Thinking (Auxiliary) – I	2) Feeling (Auxiliary) – I	2) Feeling (Auxiliary) – I	2) Thinking (Auxiliary) – I
3) Feeling (Tertiary) – I	3) Thinking (Tertiary) – I	3) Thinking (Tertiary) – I	3) Feeling (Tertiary) – I
4) Intuition (Inferior) – I	4) Intuition (Inferior) – I	4) Sensing (Inferior) – I	4) Sensing (Inferior) – I
ESTJ	**ESFJ**	**ENFJ**	**ENTJ**
1) Thinking (Dominant) – E	1) Feeling (Dominant) – E	1) Feeling (Dominant) – E	1) Thinking (Dominant) – E
2) Sensing (Auxiliary) – I	2) Sensing (Auxiliary) – I	2) Intuition (Auxiliary) – I	2) Intuition (Auxiliary) – I
3) Intuition (Tertiary) – I	3) Intuition (Tertiary) – I	3) Sensing (Tertiary) – I	3) Sensing (Tertiary) – I
4) Feeling (Inferior) – I	4) Thinking (Inferior) – I	4) Thinking (Inferior) – I	4) Feeling (Inferior) – I

E = Extraverted   I = Introverted

14
LOOKING AT TYPE AND CAREERS

police work, accounting).

Extraverts use their dominant function in their extraverted world, which is where they prefer to be. For example, if you are an ENFP, that means you like to apply your intuition to the outer world of people and things. For balance, extraverts develop their auxiliary function (second favorite) for use in their introverted world. An ENFP likes to use their feeling function in the inner world of ideas, thus their feeling function is not as readily seen by others. *Introverts* use their dominant function in the inner world of the mind, which is where they prefer to be. If you are an ISTJ, for example, you prefer to use your sensing function in the inner world of ideas. For balance, introverts develop their auxiliary function (second favorite) for use in their extraverted world. An ISTJ likes to use their thinking function on the outer world of people and things.

Your least preferred function tends to be your least well developed function. It is also called your inferior function because it tends to lag behind all of the others in its development. It is the opposite function of your dominant function, and is oriented in the opposite direction from your dominant function. For example, if extraverted feeling were your dominant function (as it is for ESFJs and ENFJs), introverted thinking would be your fourth or least well developed function.

Your least preferred function provides you with clues to areas of your life that you tend to avoid, and

---

Look at the chart again, and note below what your favorite, second favorite and least favorite functions are, and also whether you orient them to the inner (introverted) world or outer (extraverted) world:

My dominant (favorite) function is _____

and I orient it to the _____ world.
               inner/outer

My auxiliary (second favorite) function is _____

and I orient it to the _____ world.
               inner/outer

My least preferred (inferior) function is _____

and I orient it to the _____ world.
               inner/outer

involves skills you tend to have the hardest time developing. Work that draws on this function often feels boring, difficult or tiring. For example, if introverted thinking were your least favorite function, you would probably tend to avoid tasks that require a great deal of impersonal analysis of data, a critical or detached approach to people, or quiet and inwardly focused problem-solving (e.g., as in the theoretical or applied sciences, statistics, economics). You will most likely want to avoid careers that require you to *constantly* use your least preferred function.

What role might these functions play in your career choice? What kind of career areas or tasks might be easier or more difficult for you based on what you know of these functions?

_____
_____
_____
_____
_____

Your Type Development

Individuals tend to develop the four functions in a relatively predictable order through their lives. Since the order of development is also the order of preference for the functions, the type table on page 13 also shows you the order in which you tend to develop the four functions throughout your life.

Why is type development important for your career exploration? As you move through your life, your values, interests, and abilities change and broaden. This is partially due to your development of the four functions. As you begin to see which functions are being developed in your life, you can gain some understanding of your own individual needs and changing career options. Because your functions develop over a lifetime, your career values and interests may be different at midlife than they were when you were in high school. Your dominant and auxiliary functions will always be your favorite functions, but the career options you consider may broaden in later life as you develop your tertiary function, and possibly your least preferred function.

Since no career lets us spend 100% of the time using just our favorite and second favorite functions, we have to stretch at times to use our tertiary and

16
LOOKING AT TYPE AND CAREERS

least preferred functions. This stretching is good for our development, but too much stretching can be discouraging. Careers that require you to primarily use your third and least preferred functions may leave you feeling stressed and drained. This will depend somewhat on your stage of type development, but you will always want to make use of your dominant and auxiliary functions in some way, regardless of your stage of development. Think back on school subjects you have studied or jobs that you have had. Which energized you and which drained you?

For example, if you are an ISFP, you are most likely to find satisfying a career that makes use of your dominant feeling and auxiliary sensing functions. Thus, you are more likely to enjoy and feel competent in a career in which you can make use of your deep concern for people and harmony, your attention to the richness of sensory information, and your hands-on learning style. You are less likely to find satisfying a career that primarily relies on your least preferred function of thinking or your tertiary function of intuition. Thus, although you may be happy in a career where you can solve problems to directly help others, you may end up feeling stressed and drained if you are in a career that constantly asks you to solve abstract scientific or business management problems that require a more impersonal and analytical problem-solving approach.

If you are at a stage in your life when you are experiencing the need to develop and make use of your tertiary function, you may want to consider a career that will challenge you to develop the skills of that function, or possibly even your fourth function. For example, if you are an ISFP who is closer to midlife, you may want to consider a career or consider expanding your current career in a way that allows you to make greater use of your tertiary intuition, or even your least preferred thinking function. That is, you might feel the need to focus more on abstract possibilities, theories and symbols, and even feel the excitement of using your thinking to solve problems from a more objective analytical framework: you might find yourself newly enjoying games that involve strategy and logic.

Take some time to think about your stage of life and development and reflect on what role your dominant and auxiliary functions play (or could play) in your life and work. Are you primarily making use of your dominant and auxiliary? Are you at a stage where you want to pursue a career, or make a change within a career where you will be challenged to make use of your tertiary or least preferred functions? Can you fulfill the needs of your tertiary and inferior functions outside of your career (in a hobby for example)? You may also find it helpful to talk about type dynamics and development with someone who knows type.

_____
_____
_____
_____
_____

Environments (e.g., family, culture) sometimes discourage individuals from developing their favorite function, or push them to develop functions two, three, or four earlier than they normally would be interested in doing so. If you read a description of your type and it feels surprisingly on target for you, start with the expectation that your development has been on your natural path. If you aren't sure, take your doubts seriously, and explore other possibilities through reading different type descriptions and continuing to explore which preferences feel most natural for you.

Looking at Careers

The type descriptions in this section are intended to provide you with information for career exploration, not to encourage or discourage you in a given career pursuit. The careers listed with each type description are intended to suggest patterns of interest for each type, and to provide you with specific career ideas you may not have yet considered. They are *not* intended to be a list of careers that would absolutely be "right" for you. A wide variety of types are found in all careers and in any given career, and individuals of a given type are certainly found in the careers on their "less selected" list. However, they *are* found with less frequency.

Careers in the "selected most often" list have the highest percentage of that type, beginning with the highest. Careers in the "selected least often" list have the lowest percentage of that type, beginning with the lowest. Remember, also, that not all careers are represented in these lists.* If you are interested in a career in which someone with your type preferences is more rarely found, you may want to ask yourself some of the following questions:

1) How might family, friends, society, or my own pattern of interests, skills, and values be affecting my career choice?

2) Would I be called on to use functions that may not be as well developed for me? (See the dynamics and type development section.)

3) Is there a path within that career that would allow me to make natural use of my type preferences?

ISTJ

ISTJs are most likely to find interesting and satisfying those careers that make use of their depth of concentration, their reliance on facts, their use of logic and analysis, and their ability to organize. ISTJs are very often found in management careers, particularly in the areas of government, public service, and private business, and they are often found in technical and production-oriented careers as well. Their task orientation, realistic grounding, dependability, and respect for the facts often draw them to careers that call for an

---

* Career lists were compiled from the databank of MBTI records submitted for computer scoring to the Center for Applications of Psychological Type.

LOOKING AT TYPE AND CAREERS

organized approach to data, people, or things. These same qualities can also lead to their effectiveness as managers.

Their patience and dedication is often communicated to those around them as a calm composure, thus they often bring a stability to their work environment. As a result they can engender a degree of trust in others that leads to their placement in management or

ISTJ

CAREERS SELECTED MOST OFTEN

1) City Works Technician
2) Steelworker
3) Police Officer: Manager
4) Regional Utilities Manager
5) Manager: City, County, or State Government
6) Small Business Manager
7) Corrections Officer
8) Accountant
9) Manager: Public Service
10) Manager: Retail Store
11) Manager: Federal Executive
12) School Bus Driver
13) School Principal
14) Manager: Corporate Executive
15) Purchasing Agent
16) Computer Professional
17) Dentist
18) Coal Miner
19) Auditor
20) Electrician
21) Engineer: Mechanical
22) Cleaning Service Worker
23) Electrical or Electronic Engineering Technician
24) Teacher: Mathematics
25) Teacher: Trade, Industrial, or Technical
26) Military Officer or Enlistee
27) Law Enforcement, Corrections, Park Rangers, and Guards
28) Factory or Site Supervisor
29) Nursing: Administrator
30) Police Detective
31) Manager: Financial or Bank Officer
32) Computer Operations, Systems Researcher, or Analyst
33) Administrator: Social Services
34) Craft Worker
35) Engineer: Electrical or Electronic
36) Factory Worker or Machine Operator
37) Public Service Aide or Community Health Worker
38) Educational Administrator
39) Chemist
40) Personnel or Labor Relations Worker
41) Engineer: All Categories
42) Management Consultant
43) Engineer: Chemical
44) Farmer
45) Teacher: Coaching
46) Banking and Finance
47) Manager: Fire
48) Engineering or Science Technician
49) Judge
50) Physician: Pathology

CAREERS SELECTED LEAST OFTEN

1) Dental Hygienist
2) Fine Artist
3) Counselor: Runaway Youth
4) Clergy
5) Musician or Composer
6) Psychodrama Therapist
7) Psychologist
8) Teacher: Pre-School
9) Public Relations Worker or Publicity Writer
10) Suicide or Crisis Counselor
11) Clerical Supervisor
12) Religious Educator
13) Journalist
14) Restaurant Worker
15) Social Scientist
16) Minister
17) Writer
18) Speech Pathologist
19) Actor
20) Research Worker

21
LOOKING AT TYPE AND CAREERS

supervisory positions that require the overseeing of practical matters. In addition, their dedication can make them very hard to distract or discourage from a given task, an orientation that leads to thoroughness and accuracy in their work. They will also painstakingly follow through on any commitments they make. ISTJs are exceptionally practical and though they may not always agree with the goals of a work setting or institution, they do find a comfort instructure and will guarantee that procedures are followed.

These characteristics of ISTJs are also relevant to the other careers in which they are often found, careers where realistic precision and technical know-how are required. They also tend to be found in careers where detailed knowledge is required and where the work involves practical or hands-on experience. ISTJs report being attracted to careers where there is some structure, where the demands and rewards are clear, where they can take on responsibilities, and where they can work to gain status and security. In addition, they enjoy working alone, and if they must work with groups they tend to prefer smaller ones; they also like being able to prepare projects or group presentations ahead of time. ISTJs want results from their work that are tangible, and will work to perfect the efficient delivery of a service or product.

For ISTJs the job search tends to be a very thoughtful and practical process. They are excellent gatherers of job-related information, and they can be very organized and thorough in preparing application materials or in marketing themselves. Their dependability and willingness to take on responsibility will usually be communicated to others during the job search. Potential drawbacks for ISTJs in the job search may include a tendency to narrow the search too much, failure to consider unusual opportunities or job options, and a tendency to be cautious and undersell themselves. Under stress, ISTJs may become pessimistic during this process, and they may also become uncharacteristically impulsive. They may find it useful to engage their ability to be objective, and to see the importance of developing some flexibility in their interactions with others. They may also benefit from developing a healthy amount of enthusiasm and assertiveness as they engage in the job search.

Examples of careers often chosen by ISTJs include management in business or government, accounting, engineering, computer operations and

22 LOOKING AT TYPE AND CAREERS

analysis, technical/trade, teaching, police/corrections work, and skilled trade and crafts work. Other careers in which ISTJs are often found are listed on page 20.

ISTJs are found much less often in careers that are characterized by a great deal of nurturing work and/or relationship-oriented work. In addition, they are found less often in careers that require ongoing attention to more theoretical, abstract and symbolic material. They are also found much less often in careers in the arts and careers that require a significant amount of spontaneous adaptation or expressiveness in a group context. Careers in which ISTJs are less often found are also listed on page 20.

ISFJ

ISFJs are most likely to find interesting and satisfying those careers that make use of their depth of concentration, their reliance on facts, their warmth and sympathy (i.e., their emphasis on interpersonal values), and their ability to organize. ISFJs are very often found in careers that involve nurturing or healing others and also in some spiritually-oriented careers. Their sense of duty, personal commitment and practicality often draw them to careers in which they can support and be of service to others. These same qualities can also lead to their effectiveness in the helping and health-oriented careers.

Their loyalty and respect for tradition often helps create a feeling of stability in the work environment around them. In addition, their quiet warmth and tact are clearly felt by others even as they attend to their work, ensuring that organizational or work goals are met. Their willingness to take on responsibility is grounded in a very personal conclusion that the job is worth doing and is of benefit to others; they are exceptionally dependable. Once they have dedicated themselves to a job, they tend to carry it all the way through until it is done. Their pragmatism and sense of order often lead them to careers where they need to impose or maintain order on a body of information (e.g., a library) or some setting (e.g., an office). ISFJs do appreciate a degree of structure and organization in their work, and they are often found working behind the scenes ensuring that things are running smoothly.

Other careers in which ISFJs are often found also draw on this characteristic personal orientation, as well as on their capacity for precision and painstaking

23
LOOKING AT TYPE AND CAREERS

attention to detail. Thus, we see that ISFJs often tend to be found in careers that require direct personal care of others, attention to their physical or spiritual well-being, and/or some technical knowledge. ISFJs report being attracted to careers where they can be of help to others or provide some form of practical service to others, where they can take on responsibility and organize what they do, and where they can see tangible results from their work. In addition, they typically enjoy working in an environment that is stable, where they can make pragmatic use of their attention to detail, and where they can focus their attention fully on a project or person. At times ISFJs do need a place or space where they can work alone in an uninterrupted fashion, and when they do work with others they prefer working one-to-one rather than with larger groups of people.

For ISFJs the job search tends to be a very thoughtful and practical process. They are excellent gatherers of job-related information, and can be very thorough and organized in their job search, job application, or in marketing themselves. Their perseverance, stability and warmth are usually communicated to others during the job search. Potential drawbacks for ISFJs in the job search may include a tendency to overlook unusual job possibilities or options, a tendency to undersell themselves, and sensitivity to rejection. Under stress, ISFJs may feel some pessimism during this process, and they may become uncharacteristically impulsive. They can benefit from discussing their concerns with a trusted friend, and from seeing the importance of developing a larger perspective on their situation. They may also benefit from cultivating a healthy amount of assertiveness and optimism as they go about the job search.

Examples of careers often chosen by ISFJs include teaching (particularly K–12), medical fields with high patient contact (including family medicine and nursing), religious work, library careers, office and clerical work, and personal and social service work. Other careers in which ISFJs are often found are listed on the following page.

ISFJs are found much less often in careers that are characterized by a great deal of analytically-oriented technical work or work that requires ongoing attention to more theoretical, abstract, and symbolic information. They are also found much less often in careers that require continual adaptation and frequent change, and careers that require a more distant or ana-

LOOKING AT TYPE AND CAREERS

lytical approach to people. Careers in which ISFJs are less often found are also listed below.

ISFJ

CAREERS SELECTED MOST OFTEN

1) Religious Order: Lay Member
2) Licensed Practical Nurse
3) Clerical Supervisor
4) Teacher: Grades 1 through 12
5) Doctor of Osteopathy
6) School Bus Driver
7) Teacher: Pre-School
8) Administrator: Social Services
9) Teacher: Speech Pathology or Therapy
10) Teacher Aide
11) Nursing Aide
12) Librarian
13) Priest
14) Private Household Worker
15) Nursing: Public Health
16) Corrections Officer
17) Guard or Watch Keeper
18) Physician: Family and General Practice
19) Health Service Worker
20) Typist
21) Teacher: Reading
22) Food Service Worker
23) Bookkeeper
24) Medical Technologist
25) Library Attendant
26) Minister
27) Dental Hygienist
28) Registered Nurse
29) Administrator: Nursing
30) Health Education Practitioner
31) Probation Officer
32) Child Care Worker
33) Legal Secretary
34) Physical Therapist
35) Health Technologist or Technician
36) Dietitian or Nutritionist
37) Dental Assistant
38) Secretary
39) Hairdresser or Cosmetologist
40) Cashier
41) Office, Clerical, and Related Worker
42) Public Service Aide or Community Health Worker
43) Transportation Operator
44) Engineering: Aeronautical
45) Nursing: Critical Care
46) Electrician
47) Police Detective
48) Radiologic Technologist or Technician
49) Nursing: Educator
50) Nursing: Consultant

CAREERS SELECTED LEAST OFTEN

1) Marketing Professional
2) Manager: Corporate Executive
3) Human Resources Planner
4) Management Consultant
5) Actor
6) Photographer
7) Social Services Worker
8) Manager: Retail Store
9) Psychodrama Therapist
10) Sales Manager
11) Social Scientist
12) Psychologist
13) Lawyer
14) Engineer: Mechanical
15) Fine Artist
16) Manager: Federal Executive
17) Insurance Agent, Broker, or Underwriter
18) Storekeeper
19) Architect
20) Physician: Pathology

INFJ

INFJs are most likely to find interesting and satisfying those careers that make use of their depth of concentration, their grasp of possibilities, their warmth and sympathy (i.e., their emphasis on interpersonal values), and their ability to organize. INFJs are very often found in careers where creativity and tending to human development are primary activities. Their orientation to people, their confidence in their insights into the nature of things and people, and their fertile imagination often attract them to careers where they can draw out the possibilities in others. These same qualities can also lead to exceptional empathic abilities, which may seem to border on the psychic.

Their intense inner vision, ability to establish harmonious relationships with others, and their skills in written and oral communication can often draw others into supporting their goals. As a result, INFJs are often called on to provide leadership in areas that involve attending to the physical, emotional and/or spiritual needs of others. INFJs are full of idealism and lofty goals, and though not always apparent, they are intensely individualistic and private persons. They are also particularly attracted to careers that provide opportunities for philosophical reflection, and are attracted to careers where they have the opportunity to grow as well.

These characteristics of INFJs are also relevant to the other careers in which they are often found, careers where human contact and comfort with abstraction, symbols, and the imagination are required. They also tend to be found in careers in which spirituality or artistic expression form a part. INFJs report being attracted to careers where they can work with people to empower them and facilitate growth, where they can be creative and innovative, where they feel they are doing something consistent with their values, and where they can be independent and autonomous. In addition they enjoy challenges, and value the opportunity to express themselves and see the results of their vision. Although they value harmonious relations with others and they are oriented to helping people develop, INFJs definitely need a significant amount of alone time in their work that allows them to focus on the inner world of ideas and images.

LOOKING AT TYPE AND CAREERS

For INFJs the job search can be an opportunity to use their creativity as well as their organizational and rapport-building skills. They can envision job possibilities easily, and can pursue them both through their ability to connect with others and through their potential ability to be task-oriented. Their interper-

INFJ

CAREERS SELECTED MOST OFTEN

1) Director of Religious Education
2) Fine Artist
3) Priest or Monk
4) Consultant: Education
5) Psychodrama Therapist
6) Minister
7) Clergy
8) Physician: Pathology
9) Rabbi
10) Teacher: English
11) Architect
12) Priest
13) Suicide or Crisis Counselor
14) Media Specialist
15) Teacher: Art, Drama, or Music
16) Religious Order: Lay Member
17) Teacher: Foreign Language in Junior or Senior High School
18) Religious Educator
19) Physician: Psychiatry
20) Doctor of Osteopathy
21) Social Worker
22) Teacher: High School
23) Teacher: University
24) Research Assistant
25) Marketing Professional
26) Social Scientist
27) Librarian
28) Administrator: College or Technical Institute
29) Scientist: Biology
30) Teacher: Pre-School
31) Psychologist
32) Teacher: Special Education
33) Administrator: Health
34) Physician: All Specialties
35) Home Management Advisor or Home Economist
36) Public Relations Worker or Publicity Writer
37) Consultant: Management Analyst
38) Dental Hygienist
39) Speech Pathologist
40) Physician: Family Practice and General Practice
41) Medical Assistant
42) Teacher: All Categories
43) Occupational Therapist
44) Counselor
45) Storekeeper
46) Nursing: Educator
47) Medical Secretary
48) Teacher: Health
49) Pharmacist
50) Personnel or Labor Relations Worker

CAREERS SELECTED LEAST OFTEN

1) Factory or Site Supervisor
2) Surveyor
3) Childcare Worker
4) Electrical or Electronic Engineering Technician
5) Manager: Fire
6) Corrections Officer or Probation Officer
7) Farmer
8) Sales Manager
9) Manager: Retail Store
10) Steelworker
11) Police Officer: Manager
12) Police Officer
13) Manager: City, County, or State Government
14) Credit Investigator or Mortgage Broker
15) Manager: Corporate Executive
16) School Bus Driver
17) Machine Operator
18) Administrator: Social Services
19) Coal Miner
20) Manager: Financial or Bank Officer

sonal orientation, persuasiveness and insight are usually communicated to others during the job search. Potential drawbacks for INFJs in the job search include unrealistic expectations for a job, inaction, painful feelings that the job search is grueling or cheapening, and inattention to details of jobs or of the job search. Under stress, INFJs may develop a potentially adversarial attitude toward the world of work, and may get caught up in less relevant details. They may find it helpful to maintain a sense of humor as they view events from a broader, more meaningful perspective and as they develop more realistic job expectations and flexibility in dealing with the details of the job search.

Examples of careers often chosen by INFJs include all positions within all denominations of the ministry, education (including religious, foreign language and the arts), architecture, medicine, psychology, media and marketing work, counseling, and fine arts. Other careers in which INFJs are often found are listed on the previous page.

INFJs are found much less often in careers that are characterized by a great deal of technical work, attention to detail, work that requires realistic precision or production, or work that requires more business and bureaucratic management abilities. They are also found much less often in careers that require more practical hands-on or mechanical work, or careers that may involve a significant amount of interpersonal conflict. Careers in which INFJs are less often found are also listed on the previous page.

INTJ

INTJs are most likely to find interesting and satisfying those careers that make use of their depth of concentration, their grasp of possibilities, their use of logic and analysis, and their ability to organize. INTJs are very often found in academic, scientific, theoretical, and technical positions that require prolonged periods of solitary concentration and tough-minded analysis. Their task orientation, powers of abstraction, perseverance, and willingness to look at situations or systems in creative ways often draw them to careers where they can pursue the implementation of their inner vision. Their trust in their own insights, their faith that they see into the true meaning behind events, and their willingness to bring their insights into practical real-world application often communi-

LOOKING AT TYPE AND CAREERS

cate to others an impression of confidence and competence, even drivenness. Though these qualities often lead to their being placed in executive and management positions, INTJs are intensely individualistic and resist being bound to routine.

Autonomy and individual achievement are extremely important to INTJs and they are not easily

INTJ

CAREERS SELECTED MOST OFTEN

1) Architect
2) Attorney: Administrator, Non-Practicing
3) Computer Professional
4) Lawyer: Practicing
5) Manager: Federal Executive
6) Management Consultant
7) Human Resources Manager
8) Scientist: Chemistry
9) Research Worker
10) Social Services Worker
11) Engineer: Electrical or Electronic
12) Scientist: Life or Physical
13) Computer Systems Analyst, Support Representative, or Programmer
14) Lawyer or Judge
15) Photographer
16) Engineer: Chemical
17) Manager: Corporate Executive
18) Teacher: University
19) Psychologist
20) Social Scientist
21) Electrical or Electronic Engineering Technician
22) Actor
23) Sales Manager
24) Artist or Entertainer
25) Auditor
26) Musician or Composer
27) Scientist: Biology
28) School Principal
29) Administrator: College or Technical Institute
30) Writer or Journalist
31) Physician: Pathology
32) Credit Investigator or Mortgage Broker
33) Editor
34) Administrator: Student Personnel
35) Engineer: All Categories
36) Teacher: Health
37) Employment Development Specialist
38) Physician: All Specialties
39) Research Assistant
40) Engineer: Aeronautical
41) Consultant: Education
42) Manager: City, County, or State Government
43) Designer
44) Nursing: Educator
45) Dentist
46) Fine Artist
47) Teacher: Junior College
48) Rabbi
49) Administrator: General
50) Military Officer or Enlistee

CAREERS SELECTED LEAST OFTEN

1) Food Service Worker
2) Cleaning Service Worker
3) Storekeeper
4) Receptionist
5) Cashier
6) Teacher Aide
7) Corrections Officer
8) Nursing Aide
9) Physical Therapist
10) School Bus Driver
11) Police Officer
12) Typist
13) Purchasing Agent
14) Medical Assistant
15) Teacher: Speech Pathology or Therapy
16) Electrician
17) Construction Worker
18) Health Service Worker
19) Teacher: Foreign Language in Junior or Senior High School
20) Licensed Practical Nurse

deflected from a task or goal on which they have set their minds. They prefer challenge and appreciate opportunities to apply their creativity and intuitive insights, as well as chances to expand their repertoire of skills. Their intuition may also find expression in artistic endeavors or even in careers in the arts. Though not always seen, INTJs experience a strong need to engage in quiet, even philosophical reflection, prior to engaging the external tasks of their chosen field of work.

These characteristics of INTJs are also relevant to the other careers in which they are often found, careers where creativity and/or technical know-how are required. INTJs also tend to be found in careers where planning, revising, or designing for the future are involved. INTJs report being attracted to careers where they can be independent and creative, think systemically, feel challenged and feel that their work makes a difference. They pursue competence and mastery, and often will move quickly to something else once they feel they have gained a sufficient level of some skill or knowledge. Consequently, whatever career they choose must have opportunities for learning. INTJs need time to work alone, and when they work with others, they hope and expect those persons will be skilled and competent as well.

For INTJs the job search is an opportunity to use their creativity, their skills in synthesizing information, and their ability to approach the market in an organized and strategic fashion. They can usually envision many career possibilities, and can selectively target and pursue job options with their potential ability to be task-oriented. Their competence, analytical skills and insight are usually communicated to others during the job search. Potential drawbacks for INTJs in the job search include unrealistic expectations for a job, inaction, failure to be communicate warmth or diplomacy in interactions with others, and inattention to details of jobs or of the job search. Under stress, INTJs may develop a potentially adversarial attitude toward the world of work, and may get caught up in less relevant details. They may find it helpful to analyze their experience objectively as they see the need to be more realistic in their expectations about jobs and to be more flexible in dealing with the details of the job search.

Examples of careers often chosen by INTJs include law, engineering, architecture, physical and life sciences, psychology and social science, computer science, writing/editing, careers in the arts, and consulting. Other careers in which INTJs are often found are listed on page 28.

Careers in which INTJs are found much less often tend to be characterized by a great deal of nurturing work, relationship-oriented work, or work that requires practical, routinized production or delivery of services. They are also found much less often in careers that depend predominantly on hands-on work, attention to detail, and/or adherence to structures imposed by others. Careers in which INTJs are found much less often are also listed on page 28.

ISTP

ISTPs are most likely to find interesting and satisfying those careers that make use of their depth of concentration, their reliance on facts, their use of logic and analysis, and their adaptability. ISTPs are found in a variety of careers, but are most often found in careers that require a tough-minded analytical and realistic approach. Many of these careers are related to building and production, while others involve providing direct delivery of technically-oriented services. Their quiet adaptability, realistic grounding, and their willingness to critically analyze the facts often draw them to careers where they can take a pragmatic approach to problem-solving. They may also manifest a great curiosity about things, not so much in an abstract search for their meaning, but a curiosity about how and why they work and about their application.

Their keen powers of observation and their desire for a wealth of hands-on and sensory experiences often lead ISTPs to develop an exceptionally high level of skill with the tools or instruments they choose to use, whether that tool is a computer, a hammer, a spreadsheet, or a sailboat. Consequently, ISTPs are often found in fields that require a craftsman-like approach, and if the field is more scientific, they are often found in the more applied aspects of the field. They often enjoy jobs that involve a measure of adventure, though they may choose to meet that need outside of their work life, and they tend to resist too much structure.

These characteristics of ISTPs are also relevant to the other careers in which they are often found, careers where precision and technical know-how are required. Hence, ISTPs are often found in careers where mechanical understanding plays an important part, or in careers where they can use logical analysis to make sense of a variety of facts and real world problems. They are often quite skilled at making the most effective use of what is actually available, and they may make very good troubleshooters. ISTPs report being attracted to careers that are fun, where

ISTP

CAREERS SELECTED MOST OFTEN

1) Farmer
2) Military Officer or Enlistee
3) Engineer: Electrical or Electronic
4) Electrical or Electronic Engineering Technician
5) Coal Miner
6) Transportation Operator
7) Dental Hygienist
8) Construction, Warehouse, Groundskeepers and Other Laborers
9) Mechanic
10) Legal Secretary
11) Cleaning Service Worker
12) Surveyor
13) Corrections Officer or Probation Officer
14) Carpenter
15) Construction Worker
16) Steelworker
17) Cook
18) Small Business Manager
19) Physician: Pathology
20) Engineer: Mechanical
21) Craft Worker
22) Computer Programmer
23) Law Enforcement, Corrections, Park Rangers, and Guards
24) Lawyer
25) Engineering or Science Technician
26) Optometrist
27) City Works Technician
28) Media Specialist
29) Dental Assistant
30) Manager: Federal Executive
31) Machine Worker
32) Manager: Regional Utilities
33) Computer Professional
34) Physical Therapist
35) Manager: Fire
36) Engineer: All Categories
37) Administrator: Social Services
38) Lawyer or Judge
39) Manager: Public
40) Accountant
41) Manager: City, County, or State Government
42) Typist
43) Guard or Watch Keeper
44) Respiratory Therapist
45) Computer Operations, Systems Researcher, or Analyst
46) School Bus Driver
47) Storekeeper
48) Manager: Corporate Executive
49) Teacher: Adult Education
50) Teacher: Coaching

CAREERS SELECTED LEAST OFTEN

1) Police Detective
2) Director of Religious Education
3) Administrator: Student Personnel
4) Journalist
5) Consultant: Education
6) Engineer: Aeronautical
7) Clerical Supervisor
8) Scientist: Biology
9) Actor
10) Research Assistant
11) Nursing: Public Health
12) Dentist
13) Receptionist
14) Teacher: Pre-School
15) Fine Artist
16) Architect
17) Psychodrama Therapist
18) Suicide or Crisis Counselor
19) Occupational Therapist
20) Religious Order: Lay Member

LOOKING AT TYPE AND CAREERS

they can make use of their grasp of the details, where there is intellectual stimulation, where there are tangible results from their work, or where they can respond and adapt to what is happening in the present. They are also drawn to outdoor activities and/or careers that provide them with some excitement. They need time alone, are not particularly inclined to supervise others, and often choose jobs where they can work independently.

For ISTPs the job search is an opportunity to apply their analytical skills to the facts of the job search. They can pragmatically gather information on prospective jobs, and critically look at what they need to do to apply for a job or to market themselves. Their ability to adapt to the needs of the moment, take risks, and think realistically about problems are usually communicated to others during the job search. Potential drawbacks for ISTPs during the job search include a tendency to focus on the immediate present rather than on long-term job plans, difficulty in following through with job search tasks, and putting off making job decisions out of fear that something more exciting may come along. Under stress, ISTPs can feel overwhelmed as they engage in this process, and can benefit from checking the facts and realities of their situation. They can also benefit from considering what is truly of value to them, which will give them the drive to persevere and follow through on all parts of the job search.

Examples of careers often chosen by ISTPs include military or corrections work, farming, skilled trade and crafts work, mechanics, electrical/electronic engineering or technical work, computer programming, law, and accounting. Other careers in which ISTPs are often found are listed on the previous page.

ISTPs are found much less often in careers that require a great deal of nurturing work, relationship-oriented work and/or work that requires attention to more highly theoretical, abstract and symbolic material. They also tend to be found much less often in careers in the field of religion (whether ministry or education), and careers in the expressive arts. Careers in which ISTPs are less often found are also listed on the previous page.

ISFP

ISFPs are most likely to find interesting and satisfying those careers that make use of their depth of concentration, their reliance on facts, their warmth and sympathy (i.e., their emphasis on interpersonal values), and their adaptability. ISFPs are very often found in careers that allow for direct practical care of people or hands-on detail work that may require much solitude. Their realistic grounding, depth of feeling, and very personal approach to life often draw them to careers where they can help others in very pragmatic ways. Though often hidden, their warm and sympathetic nature can be felt by others who know them, and they communicate kindness in ways that make them exceptional candidates for working with people in need, children or animals. Their idealism and deep feeling make them particularly sensitive to the suffering of others.

In addition, ISFPs often have a special sympathy for things natural and they may feel quite comfortable working outdoors. Their ongoing enjoyment of the present moment and their tendency to express through action rather than words often lead to their developing a craftsman-like elegance in whatever work they have chosen. ISFPs are quietly adaptable in their work, and they tend to be the most comfortable in jobs that not only take advantage of their keen attention to detail and sense of aesthetics, but which also allow them a fair degree of freedom from restricting structures and rules.

These characteristics of ISFPs are also relevant to the other careers in which they are often found, careers where detailed knowledge may be required and where they can express their caring and concern for others in direct or indirect ways. ISFPs report being attracted to careers where they can deal with facts rather than theory, where they feel their work contributes to something that they care about, where they can work with people in generally noncompetitive situations, and where they can make use of practical action skills. In addition, they appreciate working in a supportive environment that fosters a degree of harmony, and where they can work independently to some degree, but where they can still be involved with others. Though they enjoy working with others, ISFPs are not particularly inclined to want to manage or supervise them, or to lead groups of people, though they can do so if their ideals require them to do so.

For ISFPs the job search tends to be a practical and people-oriented process. They are excellent gatherers of information, and their personal orientation

LOOKING AT TYPE AND CAREERS

can open doors for gathering information from people they know and trust. Their pragmatic people orientation, hands-on abilities, and adaptability will usually be communicated to others during the job search. Potential drawbacks for ISFPs in the job search include a tendency to overlook unusual job opportunities or options, an unwillingness to look at the long-

ISFP

CAREERS SELECTED MOST OFTEN

1) Storekeeper
2) Surveyor
3) Clerical Supervisor
4) Dental Assistant
5) Bookkeeper
6) Machine Operator
7) Cleaning Service Worker
8) Police Detective
9) Carpenter
10) Licensed Practical Nurse
11) Radiologic Technologist or Technician
12) Legal Secretary
13) Cook
14) Physical Therapist
15) Counselor: Runaway Youth
16) Waiter or Waitress
17) Medical Assistant
18) Typist
19) Police Officer
20) Food Service Worker
21) Health Service Worker
22) School Bus Driver
23) Private Household Worker
24) Nursing Aide
25) Manager: Fire
26) Lifeguard or Recreational Attendant
27) Secretary
28) Construction Worker
29) Corrections Officer
30) Computer Operator
31) Registered Nurse
32) Office Machine Operator and Clerical Worker
33) Electronic Technician
34) Health Education Practitioner
35) Teacher Aide
36) Public Health Nursing
37) Director of Religious Education
38) Laboratory Technologist
39) Library Attendant
40) Construction, Warehouse, Groundskeepers and Other Laborers
41) Engineering or Science Technician
42) Electrician
43) Teacher: Grades 1 through 12
44) Media Specialist
45) Mechanic
46) Child Care Worker
47) Health Technologist or Technician
48) Medical Technologist
49) Religious Order: Lay Member
50) Secretary: Executive or Administrative Assistant

CAREERS SELECTED LEAST OFTEN

1) Administrator: Student Personnel
2) Engineer: Chemical
3) Engineer: Aeronautical
4) Scientist: Biology
5) Dental Hygienist
6) Physician: Pathology
7) Actor
8) Research Assistant
9) Physician: Psychiatry
10) Religious Educator: All Denominations
11) Minister
12) Judge
13) Credit Investigator or Mortgage Broker
14) Administrator: Health
15) Manager: Retail Store
16) Manager: Federal Executive
17) Administrator: College or Technical Institute
18) Manager: Corporate Executive
19) Suicide or Crisis Counselor
20) Architect

term consequences of a job decision, and a tendency to undervalue their very real accomplishments. Under stress, ISFPs can become quite critical of others and feel incompetent as they engage in this process. If they notice this trend, they can benefit from attending to the more empowering facts of the situation, which may include truly acknowledging their skills and the importance of communicating them to others. They may also benefit from moderating their idealism and expectations about jobs and the job search.

Examples of careers often chosen by ISFPs include health care and service work, nursing, office or clerical work, personal service careers, skilled craft, trade and technical careers (carpenter, surveyor, radiologic technician, etc.), police/detective careers, and teaching (particularly K–12). Other careers in which ISFPs are often found are listed on the previous page.

ISFPs are found much less often in careers that are highly structured and in abstract fields such as management, engineering, and law. In addition, they are found less often in careers that require a great deal of tough-minded analysis of symbolic and technical material and where the skills of logical analysis and organization are constantly called for. They are also less commonly found in careers in the physical or life sciences, careers in the performing or fine arts, and careers in business or accounting. Careers in which ISFPs are less often found are also listed on the previous page.

INFP

INFPs are most likely to find interesting and satisfying those careers that make use of their depth of concentration, their grasp of possibilities, their warmth and sympathy (i.e., their emphasis on interpersonal values), and their adaptability. INFPs are very often found in careers where there are opportunities for creating and communicating, or where there are opportunities to help others. Their very personal approach to life, their sensitivity to people, and their willingness to look beyond what is present and obvious often draw them to careers in which they can foster growth and development in others. These qualities can also lead to an ability to quickly establish rapport with others, and the development of excellent communication skills.

Their idealism provides them with a strong sense of what constitutes the "good," especially where people are concerned. This idealism, in conjunction

LOOKING AT TYPE AND CAREERS

with their open-mindedness and tolerance, makes them exceptionally well suited to work in which a vision or understanding of human nature and potential is needed, though at times their perfectionism can hinder their work. Though human values are deeply important to the INFP, their deep feeling and warmth may not always be apparent at first meeting, and what is more likely to be seen in the external world of their career is their adaptability, their focus on possibilities and their communication skills. They may have well-developed writing or speaking skills, are often drawn to higher education, and they may have a particular affinity for languages and the arts. INFPs tend to dislike a great deal of structure or rules in their work environment, and they are usually patient with complexity.

These characteristics of INFPs are also relevant to other careers in which they are often found, careers in which the work requires quiet concentration, where they can work with people in a more private, one-to-one relationship, and/or where interpersonal sensitivity is important. They also tend to be found in careers where they can be creative or where the work they do leads to an increased understanding of the human condition and ways human suffering can be alleviated. INFPs report being attracted to careers where they can work with and develop relationships with others, particularly other creative and caring people, where they can help others, and where they feel the job has meaning and purpose. They also report being attracted to careers that allow them the flexibility to be creative, where they are intellectually stimulated, and where there is room for variety and learning. A degree of privacy and alone time in their work is usually very important to INFPs.

For INFPs the job search can be an opportunity to use their creativity, flexibility and their skills in self-expression. They can generate a variety of job possibilities, consider them for their ability to fulfill their values, and pursue them using their skills in communicating with others, either in writing or in person. Their idealism, commitment, flexibility and people skills will usually be communicated to others in the job search. Potential drawbacks for INFPs in the job search include unrealistic expectations for a job, feelings of inadequacy or lack of confidence, and inattention to the details of jobs or of the job search. Under stress, INFPs may become quite critical of others and themselves, and they may hold themselves back because they feel incompetent as they engage in this process. They can benefit from allowing their intuition to give them a new perspective on the possibilities available in the situation. They may also find it helpful to truly acknowledge their skills, as well as the importance of communicating those skills to others. In addition, INFPs can benefit from developing realistic expectations about the job search, and

INFP

CAREERS MOST OFTEN SELECTED

1) Fine Artist
2) Physician: Psychiatry
3) Counselor: Runaway Youth
4) Architect
5) Editor
6) Research Assistant
7) Suicide or Crisis Counselor
8) Journalist
9) Psychologist
10) Religious Educator: All Denominations
11) Social Scientist
12) Writer
13) Laboratory Technologist
14) Consultant: Education
15) Counselor: School
16) Laboratory Technologist or Technician
17) Physical Therapist
18) Teacher: Art, Drama, or Music
19) Carpenter
20) Restaurant Worker
21) Social Worker
22) Media Specialist
23) Counselor: Rehabilitation
24) Counselor: Vocational or Educational
25) Actor
26) Research Worker
27) Teacher: English
28) Cook
29) Scientist: Biology
30) Librarian
31) Speech Pathologist
32) Artist or Entertainer
33) Employment Development Specialist
34) Public Health Nursing
35) Musician or Composer
36) Psychodrama Therapist
37) Teacher: Reading
38) Secretary: Executive or Administrative Assistant
39) Engineer: Aeronautical
40) Surveyor
41) Designer
42) Physician: All Specialties
43) Teacher: Foreign Language in Junior or Senior High School
44) Waiter or Waitress
45) Minister
46) Clergy
47) Attorney: Administrator, Non-Practicing
48) Priest or Monk
49) Health Technologist or Technician
50) Administrator: Education

CAREERS SELECTED LEAST OFTEN

1) Police Detective
2) Manager: Fire
3) Computer Operations, System Researcher, or Analyst
4) Management Consultant
5) Purchasing Agent
6) Corrections Officer
7) School Bus Driver
8) Small Business Manager
9) Manager: Retail Store
10) Manager: Regional Utilities
11) Coal Miner
12) Police Officer: Manager
13) City Works Technician
14) Human Resources Planner
15) Social Services Worker
16) School Principal
17) Manager: City, County, or State Government
18) Sales Manager
19) Manager: Restaurant, Bar, or Food Service
20) Storekeeper

from objectively looking at the logical consequences of the various decisions they make.

Examples of careers often chosen by INFPs include fine arts careers, writing and journalism, psychology and psychiatry, social sciences, counseling, architecture, education (religion, art, drama, music, and foreign languages), library careers, acting, and entertainment. Other careers in which INFPs are often found are listed on the previous page.

INFPs are found much less often in careers that require skills and interests in management, business, factory work, and other fields requiring attention to detail, systematic logical analysis, or highly structured work. They are also found much less often in careers that require a great deal of interpersonal competition, or careers that involve a significant amount of hands-on, manual, or mechanical work. Careers in which INFPs are less often found are also listed on the previous page.

INTP

INTPs are most likely to find interesting and satisfying those careers that make use of their depth of concentration, their grasp of possibilities, their use of logic and analysis, and their adaptability. INTPs are very often found in academic, theoretical, and technical positions, many of which require prolonged periods of solitary concentration and tough-minded analysis. Their concern with ideas and their natural curiosity about the underlying principles and explanations for events often draws them to careers where an in-depth understanding of some abstract subject is required. Their abilities to become absorbed in an idea, to concentrate to the exclusion of all distractions, and to be objectively critical and creative often lead to their gaining a remarkable understanding of some complex problem, issue, or subject matter.

INTPs are drawn to careers in which problem analysis and creative solutions are required, and they may have exceptional skills in finding inconsistencies, critiquing a situation, and offering remedies. These skills apply to whatever field they have chosen, whether it is computer programming, market analysis, science, writing/editing, or law. INTPs are also often found in settings where ideas and inspiration are primary, hence they are often drawn to the academic setting, both as students and teachers. They enjoy being around those who share their own drive to understand, and as teachers, they are more inclined to work with advanced students. INTPs often have strong needs for freedom, autonomy and variety, and what is often first observed in them is their easy adaptability and creative lifestyle. INTPs tend to resist a great deal of structure and rules in their work environment, and need private time for the introspective analysis that is their hallmark.

INTP

CAREERS SELECTED MOST OFTEN

1) Scientist: Chemistry
2) Computer Professional
3) Architect
4) Research Assistant
5) Fine Artist
6) Computer Programmer, Systems Analyst, or Support Representative
7) Lawyer
8) Food Service Worker
9) Surveyor
10) Manager: Federal Executive
11) Social Scientist
12) Electronic Technician
13) Scientist: Biology
14) Writer or Journalist
15) Photographer
16) Psychologist
17) Scientist: Life or Physical
18) Actor
19) Computer Operations or Systems Researcher
20) Pharmacist
21) Respiratory Therapist
22) Editor
23) Judge
24) Business: General, Self-Employed
25) Physician: Pathology
26) Suicide or Crisis Counselor
27) Legal Secretary
28) Engineering or Science Technician
29) Engineer: All Categories
30) Counselor: Runaway Youth
31) Allied Health or Health Practitioner
32) Storekeeper
33) Attorney: Administrator, Non-Practicing
34) Dentist
35) Physician: Psychiatry
36) Physician: All Specialties
37) Factory or Site Supervisor
38) Electrician
39) Management Consultant
40) Public Relations Worker or Publicity Writer
41) Engineer: Electrical or Electronic
42) Engineer: Aeronautical
43) Teacher: University
44) City Works Technician
45) Laboratory Technologist or Technician
46) Machine Operator
47) Occupational Therapist
48) Artist or Entertainer
49) Administrator: College or Technical Institute
50) Electrical or Electronic Engineering Technician

CAREERS SELECTED LEAST OFTEN

1) Director of Religious Education
2) Consultant: Education
3) Home Management Advisor or Home Economist
4) Dental Hygienist
5) Manager: Fire
6) Cleaning Service Worker
7) Military Officer or Enlistee
8) Religious Educator: All Denominations
9) Corrections Officer
10) Typist
11) Small Business Manager
12) Teacher Aide
13) Priest
14) Hairdresser or Cosmetologist
15) Teacher: Reading
16) School Principal
17) Health Education Practitioner
18) Library Attendant
19) Sales Manager
20) Marketing Professional

LOOKING AT TYPE AND CAREERS

These characteristics of INTPs are also relevant to the other careers in which they are often found, careers where theory development is important, where the manipulation of abstract ideas or information is necessary, and that require a more objective or analytic approach to people or things. INTPs report being attracted to careers where there is a stream of new problems or situations to challenge them; careers that allow for time alone, thinking, and imagining; and careers that allow for more independence and creativity. They prefer to focus their attention on the problem-solving process rather than on end products or the realistic application of their ideas. They are less inclined to supervise or organize others, and if they do work with others, they prefer working with persons they see as skilled and competent.

For INTPs the job search is an opportunity to use their analytical skills, their creativity and their adaptability. They can conceive of a variety of job opportunities, see the long term consequences of decisions, and be innovative both in their job search and in their selling of themselves. Their critical thinking skills, ingenuity, and flexibility will usually be communicated to others in the job search. Potential drawbacks for INTPs in the job search include unrealistic expectations for a job or the job search, inaction, failure to establish rapport with others or to attend to the interpersonal requirements of the job search, and reluctance to make a decision. Under stress, INTPs can feel overwhelmed as they engage in this process, and can benefit from allowing their insight to provide them with a new idea or a new perspective on the situation. They may also find it useful to determine what is important to them, and to be sure to act and follow through on the important details of the job search. They can also benefit from considering what is truly of value to them, which will give them the drive to persevere and follow through on all parts of the job search.

Examples of careers often chosen by INTPs include physical and life sciences, computer science, social sciences, architecture, law, careers in the arts and entertainment, photography, writing and journalism, engineering, and medicine. Other careers in which INTPs are often found are listed on the previous page.

Careers in which INTPs are found much less often tend to be highly structured and detail-oriented, or require living in a highly routinized environment, such as in military or corrections work. INTPs are also found much less often in careers that involve a great deal of direct human service work or careers that require ongoing attention to people's emotional lives or daily needs, including for example the religious professions, nursing, or teaching young people. Careers in which INTPs are less often found are listed on page 39.

ESTP

ESTPs are most likely to find interesting and satisfying those careers that make use of their breadth of interests, their reliance on facts, their use of logic and analysis, and their adaptability. ESTPs are found in a variety of careers, but are most often found in careers that require an active, realistic and hands-on approach. Their realistic grounding, adaptability, and desire for contact with the world often draw them to careers in trades, business and sales, and some of the technically-oriented professions. They are inclined to put more trust in, and learn better from, first-hand experience, and they have an active curiosity about the world in which they live. Their friendliness, flexibility, and tolerance of the realities of a situation can make them quite skillful in handling interpersonal conflict. These qualities, in conjunction with their use of a more objective and analytic approach to decision-making, can make them superbly pragmatic problem-solvers and skilled in convincing or negotiating with others.

ESTPs are often found in careers that require an ongoing practical adaptation to changing circumstances; they can make excellent trouble-shooters. Their analytical skills are used on the facts of a situation, and thus they may also be very good at making use of available resources. At times ESTPs may not mind bending the rules to get something. In addition, they may demonstrate a remarkable memory for facts and details, which is related to their active willingness to be fully involved in life experiences, an involvement which can drive them to take great enjoyment in all things physical. Possible extensions of their approach to life include their becoming very skilled in the use of certain tools or instruments, and their seeking out of work where they can enjoy a degree of risk. ESTPs typically enjoy jobs that do not place too much structure or too many rules on them, and they

LOOKING AT TYPE AND CAREERS

usually need a great deal of contact with people.

These characteristics of ESTPs are also relevant to the other careers in which they are often found, careers which include public and protective service work, and personal service work. They report being attracted to careers where they can trouble shoot, explore, experiment, and have a sense of freedom. Also, ESTPs report being attracted to careers where

ESTP

CAREERS SELECTED MOST OFTEN

1) Marketing Professional
2) Police Detective
3) Carpenter
4) Small Business Manager
5) Police Officer
6) Auditor
7) Craft Worker
8) Farmer
9) Warehouse, Freight, Groundskeepers, and Other Laborers
10) Manager: Fire
11) Construction Worker
12) Public Service Aide or Community Health Worker
13) Transportation and Machine Operator
14) Storekeeper
15) Restaurant Worker
16) Guard or Watch Keeper
17) Law Enforcement, Corrections, Park Rangers, and Guards
18) Manager: City, County, or State Government
19) Social Service Worker
20) Editor or Reporter
21) Business: General, Self-Employed
22) Electronic Technician
23) Lifeguard or Recreation Attendant
24) Personal Service Worker
25) Personnel or Labor Relations Worker
26) Credit Investigator or Mortgage Broker
27) Corrections or Probation Officer
28) Banking
29) Salesperson
30) Optometrist
31) Electrician
32) Manager: Financial or Bank Officer
33) Pharmacist
34) Laboratory Technologist
35) Respiratory Therapist
36) Coal Miner
37) Mechanic
38) Computer Programmer
39) Radiologic Technologist or Technician
40) Insurance Agent, Broker, or Underwriter
41) Teacher: Adult Education
42) Engineer: Mechanical
43) Nursing: Critical Care
44) Journalist
45) Factory or Site Supervisor
46) Engineer: All Categories
47) Purchasing Agent
48) Food Service Worker
49) Consultant: General
50) Childcare Worker

CAREERS SELECTED LEAST OFTEN

1) Director of Religious Education
2) Administrator: Student Personnel
3) Engineer: Chemical
4) Surveyor
5) Consultant: Education
6) Engineer: Electrical or Electronic
7) Electrical or Electronic Engineering Technician
8) Photographer
9) Dental Hygienist
10) Food Service Worker
11) Scientist: Chemistry
12) Cleaning Service Worker
13) Research Assistant
14) Medical Assistant
15) Employment Development Specialist
16) Nursing: Public Health
17) Consultant: Management Analyst
18) Teacher: Pre-School
19) Office Manager
20) Media Specialist

they can deal with specifics, work with things that can be seen, or promote something. They also like jobs that offer them change and variety, and where they can have fun. ESTPs often enjoy responding and adapting to unplanned situations.

For ESTPs the job search is an extremely practical process. They can actively make connections with others and/or make use of past connections to gather information on jobs, they can critically and objectively look at the realities of what will be required in the job search, and they can typically sell themselves well. Their energy, adaptability and practicality are usually communicated to others during the job search. Potential drawbacks for ESTPs in the job search include a tendency to focus only on the immediate present rather than on long-term job plans, failure to consider unusual job opportunities or career paths, and failure to follow through or to communicate seriousness and dependability. Under stress, ESTPs may feel very confused or inappropriately see negative meanings in many events during the job search process. They may find it useful to engage their objectivity to analyze the realities of a situation, and they may benefit from understanding that their options are not really closed off if they develop long-range career plans.

Examples of careers often chosen by ESTPs include marketing and sales, police or corrections work, skilled trades and craft work, construction work, banking, farming, management in small businesses and government, journalism, and personal services. Other careers in which ESTPs are often found are listed on the previous page.

ESTPs are found much less often in careers that require interests or skills in the theoretical or abstract, such as engineering, architecture, social sciences, or teaching. They also tend to be found much less often in highly structured human care roles such as psychology, health care, and the religious professions. Careers in which ESTPs are less often found are also listed on the previous page.

ESFP

ESFPs are most likely to find interesting and satisfying those careers that make use of their breadth of interests, their reliance on facts, their warmth and sympathy (i.e., their emphasis on interpersonal values), and their adaptability. ESFPs are found in a variety of careers, many of which include active health and human services, such as nursing, teaching and childcare. Their warmth, enthusiasm, attention to detail, and realistic grounding often draw them to these people-oriented careers. ESFPs are also found working in many office and clerical positions as well as in some active outside jobs. They are inclined to put more trust in, and learn better from, first-hand experience, and they have an active curiosity about the world in which they live. ESFPs thoroughly enjoy being with others, and their active curiosity leads them to seek ongoing involvement not only with people, but also in all things physical.

Their realistic acceptance of the facts, their open-minded tolerance, and their tactful, sympathetic approach to others can make them exceptionally skilled in any career that requires them to meet, work with, or entertain people. They may also be quite skilled in remembering facts about the people with whom they work. ESFPs value cooperation and may also have skills in managing conflicts. Their trust of the facts and their ability to respond to the needs of the moment often translate into pragmatic problem-solving skills: they can make excellent trouble-shooters. Realists at heart, they may be comfortable bending the rules to make things work. They may also have a flair for the aesthetic and can be skilled at jobs that involve designing, molding or shaping, particularly when the work is hands-on and uses real materials. ESFPs typically like jobs that allow them freedom to be active, where there is less structure, and where there are chances to interact with a variety of people.

These characteristics of ESFPs are also relevant to the other careers in which they are often found, careers where ongoing and practical contact with people is required, where hands-on work is involved, or where some detailed practical knowledge is necessary. ESFPs report being attracted to careers that allow them to be actively involved with others, where they can serve/help/guide people, and where there is a great deal of flexibility and room for spontaneity. They appreciate excitement in their work, and they often say it is important for a job to be fun. ESFPs like to be personally involved in their work and to be where the action is; they are often naturals for group work.

For ESFPs the job search is a pragmatic process and an extension of their very personal style. They can make use of past connections with people or establish new connections easily to gather job information, and they are often excellent at selling themselves and their adaptability. Their pragmatic people orientation and people skills, their flexibility, and their command of the facts are usually communicated

ESFP

CAREERS SELECTED MOST OFTEN

1) Child Care Worker
2) Transportation Worker
3) Factory or Site Supervisor
4) Library Worker
5) Cashier
6) Designer
7) Receptionist, Clerical Supervisor or Typist
8) Lifeguard or Recreation Attendant
9) Teacher: Pre-School
10) Teacher: Coaching
11) Restaurant or Food Service Worker
12) Respiratory Therapist
13) Religious Educator: All Denominations
14) Storekeeper
15) Engineer: Aeronautical
16) Medical Secretary
17) Bookkeeper
18) Nursing: Public Health
19) Electrician
20) Clerical Worker
21) Insurance Agent, Broker, or Underwriter
22) Computer, Peripheral Equipment, or Office Machine Operator
23) Nursing Aide
24) Dental Hygienist
25) Laboratory Technologist
26) Construction Worker
27) Carpenter
28) Salesperson
29) Police Officer
30) Medical Assistant
31) Private Household Worker
32) Hairdresser or Cosmetologist
33) Counselor: Rehabilitation
34) Factory Machine Operator
35) Religious Worker
36) Teacher: Foreign Language in Junior or Senior High School
37) Nursing: Critical Care
38) Banking
39) Teacher: Elementary School
40) Teacher: Grades 1 through 12
41) Radiologic Technologist or Technician
42) Farmer
43) Social Services Worker
44) Real Estate Agent or Broker
45) Mechanic
46) Craft Worker
47) Personal Service Worker
48) Teacher: Mathematics
49) Editor or Reporter
50) Teacher: Adult Education

CAREERS SELECTED LEAST OFTEN

1) Director of Religious Education
2) Administrator: Student Personnel
3) Engineer: Chemical
4) Physician: Psychiatry
5) Management Consultant
6) Engineer: Mechanical
7) Research Worker
8) Attorney: Administrator, Non-Practicing
9) Corrections Officer
10) Human Resources Planner
11) Fine Artist
12) Architect
13) Manager: Federal Executive
14) Computer Professional
15) Credit Investigator or Mortgage Broker
16) Administrator: Education
17) Priest or Monk
18) Manager: Retail Store
19) Accountant
20) Teacher: English

to others during the job search. Potential drawbacks for ESFPs in the job search include a tendency to overlook unusual job options, lack of planning and concern with the long view in their job search, and a tendency to put off decision-making. Under stress, ESFPs may feel very confused or inappropriately see negative meanings in many events during the job search process. They may find it useful to engage their feeling to decide what is important to them, and they may benefit from understanding that their options are not really closed off if they develop long-range career plans.

Examples of careers often chosen by ESFPs include teaching (particularly pre-school through grade 12) and coaching, child care work, clerical and office work, recreational work, food service, nursing, sales, personal services, and religious work/education. Other careers in which ESFPs are often found are listed on the previous page.

ESFPs are found much less often in careers that are highly structured, theory oriented, or in high technology positions such as engineering, management, and computer sciences. They are also found much less often in careers that tend to require a more impersonal and analytical approach to people, such as social science or law, or that have very little contact with people, such as research or highly quantitative work (e.g., research, accounting, auditing). Careers in which ESFPs are less often found are also listed on the previous page.

ENFP

ENFPs are most likely to find interesting and satisfying those careers that make use of their breadth of interests, their grasp of possibilities, their warmth and sympathy (i.e., their emphasis on interpersonal values), and their adaptability. ENFPs are very often found in careers that are characterized by interests and abilities in working with people and fostering their growth, or that require skills in communication and expression, whether in oral or written form. Their interest in symbols, meaning, and human relationships often attracts them to careers where they can be active, involved with others, and/or pursue new horizons. These same qualities can also lead to their developing particular skills in understanding others and drawing out the possibilities in them. Their imagination and enthusiasm lead them to be innovative in whatever they have chosen as a career, and they are almost driven to think of new projects and new ways of doing things. Their inspirations provide them with the energy to initiate a variety of new activities, and finding solutions to problems energizes them. They do not sit still for long, if ever, due to their active involvement with the world.

ENFP

CAREERS SELECTED MOST OFTEN

1) Psychodrama Therapist
2) Journalist
3) Counselor: Rehabilitation
4) Teacher: Art, Drama, or Music
5) Counselor: Runaway Youth
6) Research Assistant
7) School Counselor
8) Psychologist
9) Director of Religious Education
10) Counselor: All Specialties
11) Clergy
12) Suicide or Crisis Counselor
13) Writer
14) Musician or Composer
15) Vocational or Educational Counselor
16) Social Scientist
17) Computer Operator
18) Actor
19) Public Relations Worker or Publicity Writer
20) Restaurant Worker, Waiter, or Waitress
21) Administrator: Student Personnel
22) Social Worker
23) Artist or Entertainer
24) Receptionist
25) Dental Hygienist
26) Engineer: Aeronautical
27) Consultant: Education
28) Surveyor
29) Speech Pathologist
30) Fine Artist
31) Insurance Agent, Broker, or Underwriter
32) Office Manager
33) Minister
34) Teacher: Junior College
35) Teacher: Health
36) Teacher: Special Education
37) Religious Order: Lay Member
38) Cashier
39) Food Service Worker
40) Priest or Monk
41) Nursing Aide
42) Religious Educator: All Denominations
43) Medical Assistant
44) Editor
45) Consultant: Management Analyst
46) Teacher: English
47) Occupational Therapist
48) Human Resources Planner
49) Teacher: Pre-School
50) Lawyer

CAREERS SELECTED LEAST OFTEN

1) Scientist: Chemistry
2) Farmer
3) School Bus Driver
4) Manager: Retail Store
5) Manager: Corporate Executive
6) Steelworker
7) Administrator: Social Services
8) Computer Systems Analyst or Support Representative
9) Sales Manager
10) City Works Technician
11) Management Consultant
12) Coal Miner
13) Physician: Pathology
14) Engineer: Chemical
15) Manager: City, County, or State Government
16) Small Business Manager
17) Transportation Operator
18) School Principal
19) Corrections Officer
20) Guard or Watch Keeper

LOOKING AT TYPE AND CAREERS

Their spontaneity, warmth, optimism, and keen interpersonal perceptions can make them exceptionally skillful in working with people, whether they have chosen to encounter others through sales, teaching, counseling, or any other people-oriented career. ENFPs may be remarkably skilled at motivating others, and usually feel at home working with groups of people. Their adaptability allows them to work with others, or in any career setting, from inspiration rather than from a plan, and they typically prefer to have relatively few rules or structures in their work environment. ENFPs can often develop skills in any field that truly interests them. Their facility with symbols and their interest in meaning and the abstract often lead them to the arts as a mode of self-expression, but their skills and interests may lead them into the sciences as well.

These characteristics of ENFPs are also relevant to the other careers in which they are often found, careers that provide opportunities to be creative, such as careers in the expressive or fine arts. ENFPs report being attracted to careers that allow for challenge and variety, and where they can work with ideas and continue to learn. They want work that they can care about, where they can work with and help people, and where self-expression and creativity are possible. They would also rather be involved in the beginning or start-up phases of a project than be responsible for detail work and follow-through.

For ENFPs the job search can be an opportunity to use their energy, creativity and adaptability. They can imagine a variety of job possibilities, make use of their wide variety of relationships to gather information about job opportunities, and market themselves with confidence. Their ingenuity, enthusiasm, and people skills will usually be communicated to others during the job search. Potential drawbacks for the ENFP in the job search include unrealistic expectations about jobs or the job search, a tendency to let opportunities pass by for lack of decision-making, and failure to be organized or to follow through on important details. Under stress, ENFPs may become withdrawn and listless, or they may become inappropriately concerned with the details of the job search. They may find it helpful to reconsider what their values are and what is important to them as they attend to the realities of the job search, and to appreciate the necessity of taking a measured approach to the job search process.

Examples of careers often chosen by ENFPs include counseling, teaching (particularly at the high school and university level), psychology, journalism/writing, social science, fine arts, acting and entertainment, music, the ministry and religious education, food service, and public relations. Other careers in which ENFPs are often found are listed on page 47.

ENFPs are found much less often in careers that require a great deal of precision and logical analysis, or careers that are highly structured or routinized, such as careers in management or in the hard sciences. ENFPs are also found less often in careers that require a great deal of hands-on work or work in isolation. Careers in which ENFPs are less often found are also listed on page 47.

ENTP

ENTPs are most likely to find interesting and satisfying those careers that make use of their breadth of interests, their grasp of possibilities, their use of logic and analysis, and their adaptability. ENTPs are found in a variety of careers that reflect their diversity of interests, but the fields in which they work typically allow them to engage their inventive and analytical minds. Their creativity, comfort with the abstract, and problem-solving abilities often attract them to careers in the fields of science, communications, and technology. They are almost driven to start new projects or envision new ways of doing things, and because they are so stimulated by complexity and new problems to solve, they are often found in careers where troubleshooting plays a part. In addition, whatever career they choose must provide them with a stream of new challenges, whether that career is in the sciences, journalism, or elsewhere. ENTPs are not inclined to sit still for long.

Competence is usually of great importance to them, and they may enjoy careers where they can continually test out their abilities to analyze, debate, convince, improvise, and succeed. ENTPs can often develop skills in any field that truly interests them. They usually have a great deal of enthusiasm and confidence not only in their ideas but also in their ability to succeed, which often translates into skill in influencing or winning the support of others. Their outgoingness, their more analytic stance, and their keen perceptions of other people can make them successful in careers that require more objective

LOOKING AT TYPE AND CAREERS

approaches to people, as in law, public relations, or marketing. They tend to be nonconformists, and their sureness in the value of their insights can serve to justify their willingness to go around the system; they may have an entrepreneurial character. ENTPs value autonomy and excitement, and usually resist having

ENTP

CAREERS SELECTED MOST OFTEN

1) Photographer
2) Marketing Professional
3) Journalist
4) Actor
5) Computer Systems Analyst or Support Representative
6) Credit Investigator or Mortgage Broker
7) Physician: Psychiatry
8) Engineer: Chemical
9) Construction Worker
10) Engineer: Mechanical
11) Public Relations Worker or Publicity Writer
12) Artist or Entertainer
13) Research Worker
14) Electrician
15) Lawyer
16) Management Consultant
17) Consultant: General
18) Manager: Corporate Executive
19) Restaurant or Food Service Worker
20) Computer Operations, Systems Researcher, Programmer, or Analyst
21) Electronic Technician
22) Engineer: Aeronautical
23) Writer
24) Corrections Officer or Probation Officer
25) Child Care Worker
26) Sales Manager
27) Psychodrama Therapist
28) Electrical or Electronic Engineering Technician
29) Scientist: Biology
30) Farmer
31) Dental Assistant
32) Lawyer or Judge
33) Personnel or Labor Relations Worker
34) Scientist: Life or Physical
35) Manager: Financial or Bank Officer
36) Speech Pathologist
37) Health Education Practitioner
38) Human Resources Planner
39) Medical Assistant
40) Engineering or Science Technician
41) Respiratory Therapist
42) Suicide or Crisis Counselor
43) Real Estate Agent or Broker
44) Engineer: All Categories
45) Psychologist
46) Attorney: Administrator, Non-Practicing
47) Insurance Agent, Broker, or Underwriter
48) Musician or Composer
49) Minister
50) Administrator: Student Personnel

CAREERS SELECTED LEAST OFTEN

1) Police Detective
2) Factory or Site Supervisor
3) Home Management Advisor or Home Economist
4) Teacher: Foreign Language in Junior or Senior High School
5) Corrections Officer
6) Fine Artist
7) School Bus Driver
8) Priest
9) Religious Order: Lay Member
10) Nursing Aide
11) Teacher: Pre-School
12) Teacher: Grades 1 through 12
13) Social Services Worker
14) Dentist
15) Library Attendant
16) Religious Educator: All Denominations
17) Optometrist
18) Physician: Family Practice and General Practice
19) School Principal
20) Medical Secretary

too many rules or too much structure in their work environment.

These characteristics of ENTPs are also relevant to the other careers in which they are often found, careers where creativity and expression in the external world are important, as in careers in the arts. They report being attracted to careers in which they can be independent and feel competent; where there is the opportunity for variety, creativity, and innovation; and where ideas are important. They also enjoy work where they can interact with many different people and where they can be action-oriented. They also prefer to leave details and follow-up to others.

For ENTPs the job search can be an opportunity to use their energy, creativity, and flexibility. They can usually imagine a wide range of possibilities, analyze what needs to be done to maximize their chances in the job search, and enthusiastically market themselves. Their enthusiasm, ingenuity, and thoughtful adaptability will usually be communicated to others in the job search. Potential drawbacks for ENTPs in the job search include inattention to the facts and details of jobs or of the job search, inattention to the emotional climate of interviews, and a tendency to allow opportunities to pass by due to lack of decision-making or follow-through activities. Under stress, they may become withdrawn and listless, or they may become inappropriately concerned with the details of the job search. They may find it helpful to objectively analyze the realities of their situation and to understand the necessity of taking a measured approach to the job search process.

Examples of careers often chosen by ENTPs include photography, marketing, public relations, journalism/writing, engineering, computer sciences, life and physical sciences, construction, consulting, acting, arts and entertainment, and law. Other careers in which ENTPs are often found are listed on the previous page.

ENTPs are found much less often in careers that require a great deal of pragmatic personal care or the fostering of relationships. For example, they are found much less often in careers in child care, teaching younger students (pre-school through grade 12), nursing, or careers in the field of religion. Careers in which ENTPs are less often found are also listed on the previous page.

LOOKING AT TYPE AND CAREERS

ESTJ

ESTJs are most likely to find interesting and satisfying those careers that make use of their breadth of interests, their reliance on facts, their use of logic and analysis, and their ability to organize. ESTJs are often found in careers that require the use of tough-minded, fact-oriented, and goal-directed analysis to provide leadership and direction, and they are often found in high numbers in management and administrative positions. Their energetic orientation to action, along with their objective and realistic decision-making style, often attracts them to these positions, and these same qualities often lead to their developing active and effective organizational and management skills. They are usually comfortable applying their standards of what is correct, efficient, and sensible to all aspects of their environment, and thus they can be very analytical and matter-of-fact in their evaluations not only of situations, but of people as well.

Their systematic approach to getting the job done and their ongoing respect for details and rules often communicate a sense of responsibility and sturdy reliability to others who feel they can be trusted to follow work through to completion. Decision-making usually comes naturally to them, but they want their decisions to be based on hard facts, and they are typically more interested in organizing what is going on in the here-and-now rather than in organizing abstract systems. ESTJs are often drawn to the useful applications of the field in which they find themselves, and thus they tend to be found in careers or career areas in which pragmatic and tangible results can be seen. They are often found in business and industry, but they demonstrate a willingness to organize and a pragmatic task-orientation regardless of their chosen area of work. Opportunities to interact with others are important to ESTJs, as are work environments that are structured and which have relatively clear lines of procedure.

These characteristics of ESTJs are also relevant to the other careers in which they are often found, careers that involve hands-on work, or work that requires a more objective approach to people. ESTJs report being attracted to careers where they can manage organizations, provide leadership, be involved in practical applications of concepts to real world problems, and achieve some success and stability. They prefer working systematically, and like working on concrete and straightforward projects where there are clear outcomes and objective standards. They like feeling productive and enjoy working with others who are also conscientious and production-oriented.

ESTJ

CAREERS SELECTED MOST OFTEN

1) Manager: Retail or Small Business
2) Manager: Fire
3) Purchasing Agent
4) Teacher: Trade, Industrial, or Technical
5) Manager: Restaurant, Bar, or Food Service
6) Police Officer: Manager
7) School Principal
8) Manager: Financial or Bank Officer
9) Factory or Site Supervisor
10) Manager: City, County, or State Government
11) Sales Manager
12) Corrections Officer
13) Public Service Aide or Community Health Worker
14) Manager: Public
15) Cleaning Service Worker
16) School Bus Driver
17) Insurance Agent, Broker, or Underwriter
18) Social Services Worker
19) Coal Miner
20) Police Detective
21) Management Consultant
22) Judge
23) City Works Technician
24) Steelworker
25) Manager: Corporate Executive
26) Administrator: Social Services
27) Farmer
28) Law Enforcement, Corrections, Park Rangers, and Guards
29) Accountant
30) Nursing: Administrator
31) Manager: Regional Utilities
32) Credit Investigator or Mortgage Broker
33) Engineer: Mechanical
34) Banking
35) Physician: Pathology
36) Military Officer or Enlistee
37) Police Officer
38) Engineer: Chemical
39) Computer Systems Analyst or Support Representative
40) Real Estate Agent or Broker
41) Auditor
42) Teacher: Coaching
43) Guard or Watchkeeper
44) Public Relations Worker or Publicity Writer
45) Cook
46) Office Manager
47) Storekeeper
48) Personnel or Labor Relations Worker
49) Craft Worker
50) Administrator: Elementary or Secondary School

CAREERS SELECTED LEAST OFTEN

1) Editor or Reporter
2) Fine Artist
3) Minister
4) Psychodrama Therapist
5) Attorney: Administrator, Non-Practicing
6) Research Assistant
7) Consultant: Education
8) Physical Therapist
9) Director of Religious Education
10) Counselor: Runaway Youth
11) Religious Order: Lay Member
12) Psychologist
13) Social Scientist
14) Suicide or Crisis Counselor
15) Teacher: Art, Drama, or Music
16) Clergy
17) Child Care Worker
18) Designer
19) Priest or Monk
20) Administrator: Student Personnel

For ESTJs the job search is a very pragmatic process and a natural extension of their approach to the world. Decision-making tends to come naturally to them, and they are efficient and thorough in their gathering of information and in their marketing of themselves. Their ability to network, their stability, and their logical and realistic approach to work will usually be communicated to others during the job search. Potential drawbacks for ESTJs in the job search may include failure to consider unusual opportunities, making decisions too quickly, and a tendency to be unaware of the interpersonal climate of interviews. Under stress, they may feel overwhelmed or become oversensitive to perceived criticisms of their competence as they engage in the job search. They may find it useful to take another look at the facts and realities of their situation, and to consider the importance of staying open to possibilities and to the roles relationships play in the job search process.

Examples of careers often chosen by ESTJs include management careers (in retail, business, restaurant, banking, public service, and government), technical/trade teaching, careers in the military, police and corrections work, social or public services, accounting, and construction. Other careers in which ESTJs are often found are listed on the previous page.

ESTJs are found much less often in careers that require a great deal of human service work or work requiring emotional care of others, such as careers in the counseling or the religious professions. In addition they are found less often in work that requires ongoing attention to more theoretical, abstract or symbolic material, or invention-oriented work. They are also found less often in careers in the arts or fine arts, journalism, or careers in the social sciences. Careers in which ESTJs are less often found are listed on the previous page.

ESFJ

ESFJs are most likely to find interesting and satisfying those careers that make use of their breadth of interests, their reliance on facts, their warmth and sympathy (i.e., their emphasis on interpersonal values), and their ability to organize. ESFJs are very often found in careers that are characterized by a great deal of communication, nurturance and people-oriented work, including teaching and spiritually-oriented positions. Their valuing of interpersonal harmony and their desire to find practical ways of working with and helping others often attracts them to these careers, and these same qualities often lead to their developing excellent skills in working with people. Their energy, warmth, and compassion suit

ESFJ

CAREERS SELECTED MOST OFTEN

1) Teacher: Grades 1 through 12
2) Receptionist or Medical Secretary
3) Hairdresser or Cosmetologist
4) Restaurant and Food Service
5) Administrator: Student Personnel
6) Home Management Advisor or Home Economist
7) Dental Assistant
8) Teacher: Speech Pathology or Therapy
9) Religious Order: Lay Member
10) Religious Educator: All Denominations
11) Licensed Practical Nurse
12) Teacher: Foreign Language in Junior or Senior High School
13) Health Education Practitioner
14) Office Manager
15) Teacher: Reading
16) Child Care Worker
17) Priest
18) Teacher Aide
19) Rabbi
20) Teacher: Adult Education
21) Health Service Worker
22) Radiologic Technologist or Technician
23) Speech Pathologist
24) Cashier
25) Private Household Worker
26) Public Service Aide or Community Health Worker
27) Minister
28) Nursing Aide
29) Secretary, Clerical, Bookkeeper, Typist, and Related Worker
30) Teacher: Elementary School
31) Office Machine Operator
32) Construction Worker
33) Teacher: Pre-School
34) Director of Religious Education
35) Personal Service Worker
36) Dental Hygienist
37) Guard or Watch Keeper
38) Teacher: Coaching
39) Factory or Site Supervisor
40) Teacher: Middle or Junior High School
41) Optometrist
42) Lifeguard or Recreation Attendant
43) Corrections Officer
44) Registered Nurse
45) Teacher: Special Education
46) Administrator: Social Services
47) Social Services Worker
48) Police Detective
49) School Bus Driver
50) Administrator: Elementary or Secondary School

CAREERS SELECTED LEAST OFTEN

1) Actor
2) Physician: Psychiatry
3) Management Consultant
4) Architect
5) Computer Professional
6) Lawyer
7) Computer Systems Analyst, Programmer, or Support Representative
8) Manager: Federal Executive
9) Electrician
10) Research Assistant
11) Manager: Fire
12) Fine Artist
13) City Works Technician
14) Manager: Corporate Executive
15) Psychologist
16) Manager: Retail Store
17) Editor or Reporter
18) Auditor
19) Social Scientist
20) Scientist: Chemistry

them to work in any field in which they have direct contact with others, and they are often skilled in promoting and supporting fellowship and harmony. Their willingness to idealize whatever they find valuable can lead to great loyalty to their organization or the people with whom they work. Tradition and community can have great meaning for them, and thus they will often work dutifully to meet the ends of the setting in which they work.

ESFJs are also orderly and attentive to detail, particularly when the details are in support of their people-values, and thus they are often found in careers in which they can be both nurturing and conscientious, as in teaching, health care, or personal services. ESFJs are much more interested in pragmatic and realistic activities, whether they are helping others or are otherwise engaged, and they have less patience for the purely abstract or theoretical. Their ability to attend to the strengths of others, in conjunction with their outgoing nature, can be a very positive influence on other people. As a result, they can be quite influential through their relationships, a skill which may be of use in whatever career area they choose, whether their interests are in sales, teaching, managing, or some other area. ESFJs usually want and need contact with others in their careers, appreciate a degree of structure in their work environment, and often adapt well to routine.

These characteristics of ESFJs are also relevant to the other careers in which they are often found, careers where they can make use of their ability to attend to and manipulate facts and details, such as office, clerical, or technical work. ESFJs report being attracted to careers that are people-oriented, where they can nurture, care for, and help others grow, and where they can be active. In addition, they like to know that their work has practical benefits, and although they appreciate cooperative and harmonious work environments, they also like exercising a degree of control and decision-making in organizing their own work.

For ESFJs the job search is a people-oriented and pragmatic process. They are able to develop networks and rely on existing relationships to aid in their gathering of information, and they can make use of their organizational skills in preparing for and following through on the search. Their enthusiasm, warmth, and conscientiousness are usually communicated to others during the job search. Potential drawbacks for ESFJs in the job search may include a tendency to make decisions or evaluations of situations too quickly, ignoring objective or long-range considerations in career planning, a tendency to overlook unusual job possibilities or options, and sensitivity to rejection. Under stress, ESFJs may become excessively critical, not only of themselves, but also of others. They may also begin seeing career problems in a black-and-white manner and have unrealistic expectations for advice from experts. They can benefit from attending to all of the facts of their situation, and from appreciating that harmony is not always necessary or possible in the job search.

Examples of careers often chosen by ESFJs include teaching (particularly K–12 and adult education), religious work (all forms of ministry and education), health care (including nursing and health education), personal service work, childcare, household and domestic services, and office and clerical work. Other careers in which ESFJs are often found are listed on page 55.

ESFJs are found much less often in careers that are characterized by a great deal of highly abstract, technical and analytic work, as in computer sciences, engineering, and physical sciences. They tend to be found less often in careers where extensive use of theory and logical analysis are required. They are also found much less often in careers where there may be low contact with people, where a more abstract, impersonal or analytical approach to people is involved, or where pragmatic outcomes are not obvious, as in the social sciences, psychology, law, and careers in the arts. Careers in which ESFJs are less often found are also listed on page 55.

ENFJ

ENFJs are most likely to find interesting and satisfying those careers that make use of their breadth of interests, their grasp of possibilities, their warmth and sympathy (i.e., their emphasis on interpersonal values), and their ability to organize. ENFJs are very often found in careers that require organization, expressiveness, and an interest in people's emotional, intellectual, and spiritual development. Their orientation to people, their desire for harmony, and their imagination often attract them to these careers, and these same qualities often lead to their developing excellent skills in understanding and working with others. Their energy, warmth, and compassion suit them to work in any field in which they have contact with others, and they are often skilled in promoting fellowship and harmony. They are willing to see the points of view of others, they are tolerant of a variety of opinions, and their enthusiasm often gives them exceptional skills in working with groups. These qualities and skills, in conjunction with their focus on possibilities for people, often draw them to the religious professions, counseling, or teaching.

ENFJs are often excellent communicators; they may have a facility for languages, and may be natural public speakers. Energetic, creative, and naturally engaging, they can be quite persuasive, and they are often found in careers where they can and do influence others; they are often called on to be leaders. ENFJs can be quite charismatic, and they are also often found in the performing arts. They usually want and need contact with others in their careers, and they not only appreciate opportunities to help others develop, but also want opportunities to do so themselves. Decisive and organized themselves, ENFJs also appreciate work environments that are organized and where they can be planful in their work.

These characteristics of ENFJs are also relevant to the other careers in which they are often found. They tend to have a great curiosity for ideas, are comfortable with the abstract and symbolic, and are often drawn to careers where creative or artistic expression form a part. This is particularly true when the ideas and symbols can be used to make a difference for people. They report being attracted to careers where they can establish relationships in a supportive environment, where they can help others grow and develop, and where they can work with groups. In addition they enjoy opportunities to be creative, and to feel challenged, and they like being able to make their own decisions. ENFJs report that they prefer to avoid work that requires too much attention to detail and factual accuracy.

For ENFJs the job search is a natural extension of their energetic, people-oriented, and organized style. They are able to see a variety of job possibilities, develop a job search plan, and develop and rely on existing networks in gathering information and in marketing themselves. Their enthusiasm, their people and communication skills, and their creativity are usually communicated to others during the job search. Potential drawbacks for ENFJs in the job search may include a tendency to make decisions or evaluations of a situation too quickly, inattention the details or facts of jobs or of the job search, and a tendency to take rejection personally. Under stress, they may become excessively critical, not only of them-

ENFJ

CAREERS SELECTED MOST OFTEN

1) Director of Religious Education
2) Minister
3) Clergy
4) Home Management Advisor or Home Economist
5) Rabbi
6) Priest or Monk
7) Teacher: Health
8) Psychodrama Therapist
9) Actor
10) Teacher: Art, Drama, or Music
11) Suicide or Crisis Counselor
12) Fine Artist
13) Counselor: Runaway Youth
14) Counselor: School
15) Teacher: English
16) Consultant: General
17) Optometrist
18) Musician or Composer
19) Counselor: Vocational or Educational
20) Teacher: Foreign Language in Junior or Senior High School
21) Counselor: All Categories
22) Artist or Entertainer
23) Religious Worker: All Types and Denominations
24) Dental Hygienist
25) Library Attendant
26) Physician: Family Practice and General Practice
27) Designer
28) Child Care Worker
29) Nursing: Consultant
30) Physician: Psychiatry
31) Teacher: High School
32) Writer or Journalist
33) Nursing: Educator
34) Marketing Professional
35) Administrator: Elementary or Secondary School
36) Pharmacist
37) Health Education Practitioner
38) Psychologist
39) Administrator: Education
40) Food Service Worker
41) Teacher: University
42) Teacher: Pre-School
43) Religious Order: Lay Member
44) Librarian
45) Public Relations Worker or Publicity Writer
46) Teacher: Junior College
47) Administrator: Student Personnel
48) Teacher: Middle or Junior High School
49) Social Scientist
50) Physical Therapist

CAREERS SELECTED LEAST OFTEN

1) Restaurant Worker
2) Factory or Site Supervisor
3) Computer Operations, Systems Researcher, or Analyst
4) Farmer
5) Social Services Worker
6) School Bus Driver
7) Small Business Manager
8) City Works Technician
9) Manager: Retail Store
10) Coal Miner
11) Manager: Corporate Executive
12) Steelworker
13) Manager: Regional Utilities
14) Corrections or Probation Officer
15) Personnel or Labor Relations Worker
16) Police Officer
17) Purchasing Agent
18) Military Officer or Enlistee
19) Construction Worker
20) Medical Secretary

selves, but of others. They may also begin seeing career problems in a black-and-white manner and have unrealistic expectations for advice from experts. They can benefit from allowing their intuition to provide a broader, more meaningful perspective on their situation, and from appreciating that harmony is not always necessary or possible in the job search.

Examples of careers often chosen by ENFJs include religious professions (in all denominations and areas of service, including religious education), teaching, counseling and psychology, acting, music, fine arts, writing and journalism, library work, and health care professions (including family practice medicine, nursing, and health education). Other careers in which ENFJs are often found are listed on the previous page.

ENFJs are found much less often in careers that require interests or skills in business or technical analysis, attention to detail, or hands-on precision trade work, as in engineering or computer operations. They are also found much less often in careers that involve a great deal of interpersonal conflict (as in police or corrections work), administrative work or business management (particularly if that work is not related to a people-oriented profession), or careers that have a low level of contact with people. Careers in which ENFJs are less often found are also listed on the previous page.

ENTJ

ENTJs are most likely to find interesting and satisfying those careers that make use of their breadth of interests, their grasp of possibilities, their use of logic and analysis, and their ability to organize. ENTJs are very often found in careers that require drive, leadership, innovation, and tough-minded analysis; hence, they are often found in management and leadership positions. They are often very aware of power and status issues. Their orientation to decision-making and action, and their determination to make things happen often attract them to these careers, and these same qualities can also lead to their developing skills in managing and systematically achieving goals they have set. They are usually comfortable applying their clear sense of what is correct, efficient, and effective to all aspects of their environment, and thus they can be very analytical and matter-of-fact in their evaluations not only of situations, but of people as well.

Their approach to other people tends to be more impersonal, and they value competence in others, even as they value it in themselves.

Their orientation to the big picture and future goals, in conjunction with their drive to establish structure and achieve, often results in their being found in positions where they can make policy, plan for the future, and take on responsibility. Logic rules for ENTJs, and they expect the world to make sense. This analytic stance, combined with their focus on symbols, theories, and the abstract often attracts them to careers in the sciences, particularly the physical sciences, though they are found in the social sciences as well. Whatever career area they have chosen, they are often oriented to problem-solving, and they enjoy the challenge of analyzing a complex issue and discovering a new and creative solution. In general, opportunities to interact with others are important to ENTJs, as are work environments that are structured and organized.

These characteristics of ENTJs are also relevant to the other careers in which they are often found, careers where they can make use of their creativity as well as their appreciation for ideas and complexity. They are found not only in technical positions but also in some arts-related careers as well. They report being attracted to positions that are challenging and action-oriented, where there are opportunities for leadership, where they can seek new solutions to problems, and where they can be self-determined. In addition, ENTJs enjoy work where they can engage in long-range planning, where they can feel and demonstrate their competence, and where there are opportunities for advancement.

For ENTJs the job search is an opportunity to use their analytic and planning skills, and their ability to approach the market in an organized and strategic fashion. Decision-making comes naturally to them, and they are able to make use of networks to gather information and to achieve their career search goals. Their drive, problem-solving abilities, competence and willingness to take charge are usually communicated to others during the job search. Potential drawbacks for ENTJs in the job search may include making decisions too quickly and without enough information, a tendency to ignore the interpersonal climate of interviews, failure to communicate diplomacy in interactions with others, and impatience with the details of the job search. Under stress, they may

LOOKING AT TYPE AND CAREERS

LOOKING AT TYPE AND CAREERS

feel overwhelmed or become oversensitive to perceived criticisms of their competence as they engage in the job search, and they may find it useful to consider alternative explanations or to find a larger perspective on their situation. They may also find it useful to consider the importance of patience and of staying open to the roles relationships play in the job search process.

Examples of careers often chosen by ENTJs include a variety of management and administrative positions, business and finance, marketing, psychology and social sciences, law, physical and life sciences, teaching (particularly at the university level), consulting, human resources, acting, and computer sciences. Other careers in which ENTJs are often found are listed on the following page.

ENTJs are found much less often in careers that require ongoing attention to the spiritual, emotional or personal needs of others, or that require high levels of pragmatic nurturance, including for example religious professions, nursing, or teaching young people. They are also found much less often in careers that involve providing domestic or personal services, or that require a great deal of detail-oriented clerical work. Careers in which ENTJs are less often found are also listed on the following page.

LOOKING AT TYPE AND CAREERS

ENTJ

CAREERS SELECTED MOST OFTEN

1) Management Consultant
2) Attorney: Administrator, Non-Practicing
3) Human Resources Planner
4) Computer Operations, Systems Analyst, or Researcher
5) Sales Manager
6) Manager: Corporate Executive
7) Credit Investigator or Mortgage Broker
8) Marketing Professional
9) Personnel or Labor Relations Worker
10) Administrator: Colleges or Technical Institutes
11) Administrator: Health
12) Consultant: Education
13) Consultant: General
14) Employment Development Specialist
15) Scientist: Biology
16) Research Assistant
17) Psychologist
18) Social Scientist
19) Engineer: Chemical
20) Social Services Worker
21) Manager: Federal Executive
22) Business: General, Self-Employed
23) Corrections Officer or Probation Officer
24) Scientist: Life or Physical
25) School Principal
26) Manager: Retail Store
27) Scientist: Chemistry
28) Administrator: Student Personnel
29) Auditor
30) Actor
31) Manager: Financial or Bank Officer
32) Teacher: University
33) Manager: Restaurant, Bar, or Food Service
34) Dentist
35) Teacher: Reading
36) Designer
37) Lawyer or Judge
38) Administrator: Education
39) Computer Programmer, Support Representative, or Related Worker
40) Psychodrama Therapist
41) Fine Artist
42) Technician: Electrical or Electronic Engineering
43) Physician: Family Practice and General Practice
44) Manager: City, County, or State Government
45) Administrator: Elementary or Secondary School
46) Photographer
47) Teacher: English
48) Accountant
49) Nursing: Consultant
50) Physician: Pathology

CAREERS SELECTED LEAST OFTEN

1) Police Detective
2) Director of Religious Education
3) Factory or Site Supervisor
4) Clerical Supervisor
5) Cleaning Service Worker
6) Guard or Watch Keeper
7) Bookkeeper
8) School Bus Driver
9) Religious Order: Lay Member
10) Typist
11) Hairdresser or Cosmetologist
12) Physical Therapist
13) Dental Assistant
14) Cashier
15) Priest
16) Food Service Worker
17) Manager: Fire
18) Cook
19) Child Care Worker
20) Journalist

LOOKING AT TYPE AND CAREERS

Gathering More Information

After reading your type description, you may have some more ideas about career options. Types tend to differ in the kinds of activities they like to use in finding out more about the careers in which they are interested. Not surprisingly, each type tends to manifest its own strengths and weaknesses in this regard.

Below are listed some of the activities that may be the most natural for each type.

EXTRAVERTS
- Activities that involve interacting with others.
- May tend to seek direct experience through interviewing, volunteering, or interning

INTROVERTS
- Activities that involve reflection.
- May tend to read career materials first, before seeking direct experiences or interactions with others.

SENSING TYPES
- Gather facts about potential careers, through reading if they are introverts, or through interviewing if they are extraverts.
- SFs may trust information gathered from persons they trust and respect.
- STs may trust information gathered through their analysis of the facts.
- Hands-on experiences such as interning or volunteering (especially ESs).
- May pay more attention to the facts about various careers (e.g., jobs available, salaries, location).
- May overlook the patterns of values, interests, and skills that contribute to their career development.
- May overlook careers that don't fit with their history.

INTUITIVE TYPES
- Look for patterns/meaning in the information they have, through reading if introverts, or through discussion if extraverts.
- May be more willing to trust "hunches."
- NFs may be most concerned with the possibilities for their growth in a job.
- NTs may be the most inclined analyze and compare themselves for "fit."
- May be more inclined to trust their perceptions of the possibilities and distant future goals.
- May miss important factual material in their exploration.
- May miss information available through actually trying something out.

continued on following page

Which activities are you most inclined to use? You will want to start with activities that are consistent with your natural strengths. However, you will also want to gather career information using methods that may not be as natural for you, just to be sure you give yourself the best chance of finding out which careers may or may not fit for you. Take a moment to note what activities you will use.

_____
_____
_____
_____

THINKING TYPES
- May like to work through analyses of their interests, skills, and other information.

- May use reference materials and job analyses of various occupations (especially ITs).

- May miss information available from significant others or people they trust, or may not trust that they just care about something.

FEELING TYPES
- May trust and make use of information gathered from others, or through direct experiences with others (e.g. shadowing).

- May be more inclined to make use of formal or informal counseling for career concerns, particularly if they like and trust their counselor.

- May overlook information available in more objective forms (e.g., library).

JUDGING TYPES
- May come to closure prematurely and may benefit from continuing to gather information, even if the information seems inconsistent with their initial direction.

PERCEIVING TYPES
- May feel that they continually need more information before they can make a decision, and may need to make some judgments about information they have already collected.

Looking at Decisions

After you have gathered information on yourself and on careers, you need to make some decisions about what career(s) you are going to explore or pursue further.

Sensing, intuition, thinking, and feeling all come into play in looking at career decisions, and in applying the following Zig-Zag model you learn to make better use of all of them. In doing so, you use your tools of perception (sensing and intuition) to see all aspects of our situation, and your tools of judgment (thinking and feeling) to make decisions based on both objective and subjective criteria. The chart below shows you how.

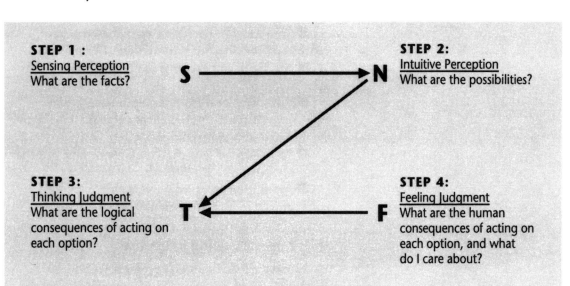

From *People Types and Tiger Stripes* (3rd ed.). Copyright 1993 by Gordon Lawrence.

At this point, think about some part of the career exploration process about which you need more clarity. Keep that issue in mind as you go through the following steps of the Zig-Zag. You may find it helpful to write down your ideas or discuss them with someone else as you go through the four steps.

Step One: Sensing Perception

You use sensing to determine the facts, data, and givens in a situation. You use sensing to face the realities of whatever career issue is before you. Below are some questions that can help you use your sensing perception.

- How are things now?
- What is your MBTI type? What are your values, interests, skills? What education do you have?
- What work activities have been most satisfying/frustrating?
- What is your job history?
- What jobs and salaries are currently available?

Step Two: Intuitive Perception

You use intuition to look at the possibilities in a situation, and/or ways to change a situation. You use intuition to notice meanings and patterns in the career information you have, and to put it in the context of your life and your future. Below are some questions that can help you use your intuitive perception.

- What do you become aware of as you open your mind to patterns in the information you have?
- Are there any patterns in the careers you consider or reject?
- What new or different possibilities come up when you set aside the belief that you are considering the one and only right thing?
- Are there options that keep coming to you that make no sense but are difficult to discount?
- Are there better ways to capitalize on your assets and to reduce your liabilities?

Step Three: Thinking Judgment

You use thinking to make a critical and impersonal analysis of the situation: the career facts and career possibilities you discovered in the past two steps. You use thinking to look at all of the consequences, both good and bad, of the various choices you have available to you. Below are some questions that can help you engage your thinking judgment.

- If you step outside of yourself and the situation, what do you see objectively and critically?
- Based on your knowledge of yourself, how well or how poorly would you fit in the careers you are considering?
- What would be the positive and negative consequences of acting on each career possibility on your list? In other words, what are the logical outcomes of choosing each career?

■ Are you able to be hard-headed about options that involve ideas or people you care about? It's important to be critical and objective in areas where you are least likely to be so.

Now that you have stepped outside yourself, it's time to reintroduce the personal element into the decision-making process.

Step Four: Feeling Judgment

You use feeling to weigh how much you care about the possible outcomes of the different career options, and what each choice means to you personally. You use feeling to give weight not only to your personal values, but also to the values and feelings of those about whom you care. Below are some questions that can help you engage your feeling judgment.

■ What do you care about in your life and career? What is important to you?

■ As you look at your options, does a part of you quickly say: this is right or wrong; this is good or bad?

■ If you acted on each possibility on your list, what would be the effect on you, on other people important in your life, and on your relationship with them?

■ What careers do you really care about, even if you think it is illogical for them to seem so important? Take what you care about seriously.

The most well-informed decisions come from using all four of these steps. However, different types are inclined to emphasize some steps, and skim over or ignore others. The type dynamics chart on page 13 will tell you which steps are likely to be the easiest for you (the steps that use your dominant and auxiliary), and which are likely to be the most difficult for you (the steps that use your tertiary and least preferred functions). For example, for an INFP, the feeling and intuition steps would likely be easier, and the lesser preferred sensing and thinking would make those steps harder. It is important to pay attention to the steps which you are most likely to skip. Many decisions are less than perfect, but the Zig-Zag will give you a clearer understanding of the road you are following so that the next steps toward your career goals will be clearer.

LOOKING AT TYPE AND CAREERS

Looking at What's Next

Setting Goals and Taking Action

Once you have made some career decisions you need to move to the planning and action steps. These next steps usually involve three things: (1) setting your career goals, (2) breaking those goals down into smaller goals and tasks, and then (3) acting on those subgoals.

Step One — Set your career goals

In this step you clarify where you are going. Long-term career goals you set in this step might include:

- broad or specific career goals, for example:
    — mechanical engineer working for an airline
    — police detective in a large city
    — salesperson for an import auto dealer
    — carpenter working for a small company that does residential work

At this point what are your long-term career goals? What career(s) do you want to pursue, or would you rather make changes within your current career?

_____
_____
_____
_____

Step Two — Break your goals down into smaller goals and tasks

In this step you determine what subgoals you need to complete and things you need to do in order for you to reach your longer-term goals. For example, some of the subgoals and tasks for the person pursuing a career in engineering could include:

- learn more about the specific areas of mechanical engineering
- find out what courses are required to get into an engineering program
- gather information on specific companies
- write a resumé and cover letters and set up interviews

At this point what are your subgoals? That is, what are other short-term goals you have to reach and tasks you have to carry out before you can reach your long-term goals?

_____
_____
_____
_____

Step Three — Take Action

In this third step you get energized to take action to reach your subgoals. In general, taking action would involve actually making those telephone calls, going on information interviews, filling out job applications, writing resumés, getting training, marketing yourself, meeting with an employer to discuss changing your current job, or taking the steps needed to create your own job.

Get going! Remember, there is a time to reflect (Introversion) and a time to act (Extraversion). Make a commitment and begin acting on your subgoals now.

Below is a list of strengths and blindspots that may be associated with your type preferences as you go through these planning and action steps.

EXTRAVERSION

Strengths
- ☐ May network naturally and already have access to a large network
- ☐ May move readily to the action phases
- ☐ May come across well in verbal interviews

Blindspots
- ☐ May discuss the career exploration process too much with others
- ☐ May act too quickly without reflecting
- ☐ May talk too much and not listen enough in interviews

INTROVERSION

Strengths
- ☐ May plan and set goals well
- ☐ May look reflective and concerned with precision as they answer interview questions
- ☐ May present self well in writing

Blindspots
- ☐ May stay too long in the reflecting and planning stages and not spend enough time acting on ideas
- ☐ May appear too reserved or serious in interviews
- ☐ May isolate themselves and not seek input from others

continued on following page

SENSING

Strengths

- ☐ May make good use of a structured career plan and subgoals

- ☐ May have a good understanding of the reality issues of a career (e.g., educational/occupational requirements, salaries, etc.)

- ☐ May remember and make use of data and facts well, both in planning and in interview

Blindspots

- ☐ May get locked in to one perception of how career exploration is to be approached

- ☐ May have difficulty seeing alternatives when feeling stuck

- ☐ May focus too much on past experience as the sole predictor of future options

INTUITION

Strengths

- ☐ May become very enthusiastic about career possibilities

- ☐ May be very good at setting up long-term goals and envisioning steps for getting there

- ☐ May be good at seeing alternatives to traditional career search and development paths

Blindspots

- ☐ May see too many possibilities and take too long to see "you can't get there from here"

- ☐ May underestimate or leave out important pragmatic steps in setting and achieving goals

- ☐ May have difficulty answering interview questions asking for specifics of job training and job history

continued

THINKING

Strengths
- ☐ May be willing to weigh all the options — even the unpleasant ones
- ☐ May approach the job search in a strategic manner
- ☐ May be good at standing their ground in a tough interview

Blindspots
- ☐ May not consider whether or not they would really like a job
- ☐ May ignore useful information if the interviewer does not meet their expectations of competence
- ☐ May appear too task-oriented in the interview and not sensitive to any interpersonal concerns involved in the position

FEELING

Strengths
- ☐ May be willing and able to make use of networks and relationships
- ☐ May be able to make good use of information interviews
- ☐ May present in interview as warm, sensitive, and personal

Blindspots
- ☐ May expect personal contacts to win a job
- ☐ May take tough interviews personally
- ☐ May present in interview as too warm and not as someone who is task-oriented

JUDGING

Strengths
- ☐ May be good at planning tasks and subgoals for reaching goals
- ☐ May be good at meeting deadlines and achieving tasks
- ☐ May communicate a willingness to take on responsibility

Blindspots
- ☐ May be impatient with the gathering of information and move to premature closure
- ☐ May adhere too closely to career goals and tasks and not see new information
- ☐ May appear too structured in an interview

continued

LOOKING AT TYPE AND CAREERS

PERCEIVING

Strengths
- ☐ May be able to respond to the need for changing plans and tasks as their career search proceeds
- ☐ May be open to see and act on options that others miss
- ☐ May be more spontaneous in their interviewing style

Blindspots
- ☐ May continue to gather information when they really need to make decisions
- ☐ May not appreciate that some career tasks may need to be completed by certain deadlines
- ☐ May seem too flexible and not goal-directed enough in interview

Selling Your Differences

One of the basic lessons of psychological type is that people of different types have different and equally valuable talents. Further, those differences are advantageous and can be used in constructive ways. From this perspective, individual differences become selling points as you go about the action stages of your career search. The purpose of this section is to help you recognize and respect your strengths, and to encourage you to sell your differences.

Whether you are looking for your first job or changing careers in midlife, you will need to sell yourself. That is, you will need to be able to assess your own personality and skills, and communicate your strengths clearly to others. Selling yourself means building on the natural strengths of who you are.

How do you identify and sell your differences? One way is to build on what you now know about type. You can look back at the descriptions given for the preferences, look at the individual type descriptions, and use type language to identify and communicate your strengths. This information is useful in filling out applications, in writing resumés or cover letters, or in interviewing.

For example, an ISTJ might say:

"I become very dedicated to my work and I am very task-oriented."

"I like responsibility and I am thorough in my work."

"I have a great respect for the facts, and I attend to the bottom line to determine if a job is done."

In contrast, an ESFP might sell different strengths with the following statements:

"I have excellent people skills."

"I take a realistic and pragmatic approach to solving problems, and I am very good at trouble-shooting."

"I am a team player, and can be very good at managing conflict at work."

As you can see in the examples above, each person is communicating about a different set of skills, yet each is communicating being a skilled and worthwhile person with whom to work. Remember, you bring your own natural set of gifts to a career.

If you have worked through the sections of this booklet, then at this point you have been through some of the major steps of the career exploration process. You have looked at yourself through the dimensions of type, values, interests, skills, and type dynamics/development. You have seen some of the career patterns for your type, and you have gathered information on careers that interest you. You then saw how type plays into decision-making and you have seen how type can affect your planning and taking action.

If you have worked through some (or all) of these steps, you are a lot further along than when you started. Congratulations! Now ask yourself if you are really through yet. It is important to stop and evaluate how this process has worked for you. Does it feel right and has it provided you with what you needed for now? You can always cycle back and gather more information on both yourself and prospective careers, and then you can make even more informed decisions, and take even more relevant action. You may also decide to seek the services of a career counselor to help you through some of the steps of your career exploration, decision-making, planning, and taking action.

At the back of this book you will find a list of further resources for looking at yourself and careers from the perspective of psychological type. Best wishes in your career pursuits!

Further Resources

There are a number of good resources for further information on psychological type and the application of psychological type to career exploration.

Do What You Are by Paul D. Tieger and Barbara Barron-Tieger. Boston: Little, Brown and Company, 1992.

Gifts Differing by Isabel Briggs Myers with Peter B. Myers. Palo Alto, CA: Consulting Psychologists Press, Inc., 1990.

Lifetypes by Sandra Hirsh and Jean Kummerow. New York: Warner Books, 1989.

People Types and Tiger Stripes (3rd edition) by Gordon D. Lawrence. Gainesville, FL: Center for Applications of Psychological Type, 1993.

Type Talk by Otto Kroeger with Janet M. Thuesen. New York: Delacorte Press, 1988.

Type Talk at Work by Otto Kroeger with Janet M. Thuesen. New York: Tilden Press, 1992.

For further information on the Myers-Briggs Type Indicator or to purchase these books, you may contact:

Center for Applications of Psychological Type
2815 N.W. 13th Street, Suite 401
Gainesville, Florida 32609
(904) 375-0160